FOR MARY. MY MOTIVATING MENTORING MAGICAL MERMAID.

My friend xx

Foreword

I was a midwife, I am the mother of 4 beautiful adults, I was the mother of a beautiful boy who left me after 6 months, I was the mother of a baby who left me before it was born. All of this has shaped me into who I have become….life experiences do that to a person, teaches us, shapes us.

Humans are, generally, strong and resilient however we all have our limits of endurance then again, even after reaching them, we still 'go on'. We learn to live our lives, with the pain. We learn to love and hope and dream again, despite our losses.

This book, short but poignant, shows us just how resilient we can be and all the possibilities that face us, even from our darkest place.

Love and light to you all, whatever your story xx

Alice McKigen-Gould

BSc, RGN, RM

WHAT TO EXPECT WHEN YOU'LL NEVER BE EXPECTING

BY

C.S. FLEUR

AN OPENING NOTE, TO YOU MY DEAR READER.

I should start off by explaining that I am not a Doctor.

I'm just a regular woman with a lived experience.

If you have been touched so profoundly by this subject

that you should seek out a book to help yourself or

someone that you love through this difficult journey,

then let me thank you for choosing my book and sharing

my story. To tell is to offload, so you reading this, helps

me to feel that if the old saying is anything to go by, my

problems shared might be halved. We can but hope.

I want to reassure you that, although you might feel

you have found a mixed bag of absolute mayhem right

here, and that might put you off, you might put it back

down because my chaos is too much for you amongst

your own at this time. That's really ok but please know, I

am a warm and loving person, and I came through later

in life ok. Underlying within all the chaos, and sadness and funny bits, and catastrophically mortifying parts, my most important message is that in the agony of it all, you aren't alone.

I send out all of my absolute love to you. No matter your circumstances, no matter the situation you are in or have been through, it is genuinely the most painful thing, in so many different and unexpected ways. The battle with miscarriage or not being able to conceive or carry, being able to conceive but not carry, or just, for whatever reason not being able to have children when the societal norm is that people generally just do or can. You might decide halfway through to hate me for my honesty, for saying the things you don't want to or can't bear to hear, but I am with you, I stand alongside you, amidst my own pain and heartache, I share all of my love with you.

You aren't alone, and neither am I.

We are one in four.

I'm writing this under a pen name not because I'm ashamed of my struggle, But because it's so deeply and profoundly personal and painful. The kind of pain which you didn't know was in existence. It leaves you questioning your sanity. It's such a raw and private experience and it isn't that I don't want to share it, I do, I want to be open and honest and helpful to other people in my shoes, it's just that I have to choose.

I struggle to open up to those closest around me about this topic. The vault stays locked. I might oblige if someone asks a question, but if they open the box fully without warning me, what I share with them will be minimal. Clinical, even. No emotion there.

And that's totally understandable, nobody wants to open the box. Ripping off the plaster from a situation where you already feel immense discomfort. This topic is not a comfortable one. Attached to it are all kinds of hideous mixtures of emotional and chaotic feelings.

The other reason is, and I really want you to consider this deeply.

By using a pen name, you don't know who I am.

This means that if I'm in the supermarket, walking my dog, in a bar having a drink with my husband or friends, if you slow your car on the street to allow me to cross, I could be that lady. I could be C.S. Fleur. Together we are all these ladies, wandering around carrying the same weight.

And we don't know who we are. I could be any one of these people, any one of these average everyday people, and I am just that, actually.

You see, there is no label on our heads. There isn't a giant stain of bright red dye on us which everyone can see, although we might feel like there is. It's a silent pain. Looking at us, a stranger cannot see our struggle. It's true with any topic. You never know what someone is going through in life, and I am a firm believer in "be kind."

But the truth is, it's an awful, sad, dark terrible subject which nobody really ever gives the green light to talk about, and what I want to do is change that. Because it is horrific and one in four women has it happen to them, and one in four women have family, partners, friends, and often other children who were also excited and looking forward to a new baby in the family, and they can't talk about it either.

The silence is deafening.

It was for me then, and it still is now, today.

Please help me change that.

In this book I won't keep the plaster on. I will open up. I'm going to talk to you about what happened in my journey, and I want you to feel free to reach out amongst yourselves and talk about your own journeys.

Use mine as an ice breaker.

With love

Chloe xx

CHAPTER ONE
The End.

2018

This book came about because of a conversation I had with my husband one night. Laid there in the dark beside him, a few words quietly crept out of me.

"Adam?" Checking he was still awake.

"Yes sweetheart?" A voice like velvet, he's so bloody lovely.

"If I'm never going to have any children, and I don't make anything, I don't have a big important career and I'm worried that when I die, it will be like I never existed. Other people have children and grandchildren. Well, I'm not going to have that, and my brother isn't going to have any babies, so I won't even be an auntie. I'm scared that I won't leave anything permanent. I'll be forgotten. It will be as if I was never even here, and it worries me. I want to be remembered for something."

You know when you say something out loud it becomes much more real? I think that's why sometimes people don't talk about their quiet terrors, because if they say the words out loud, then it's more real, and nobody wants to accept painful realities. Who can blame them?

Why do I have late night fears like these, purely because I can't reproduce? I never imagined that my situation would leave me questioning my own existence, but it does. If I had overheard another woman saying these things, I'd be absolutely heartbroken for her. I'd want to make her feel better, reassure her, or give her a cuddle and a big glass of wine at the very least.

As I write this, I'm starting to feel a little bit pathetic, to be honest. What the hell?

I'm quite sure that I'm not the only woman in the world who has had these thoughts, but I'm going to write mine down.

I'm not particularly good at writing. Especially since the stroke. Yes, a third of the way through writing this book, at 39, I had a stroke. More on that later, unsurprisingly.

Maybe **this** is what I can leave behind. Hopefully, my words here can help just one person who may be going through something similar. Maybe it will help me too, quiet the 3am terrors.

So, this book is about me, and my feelings about not ever being able to have children.

I'm a regular woman, whatever that means. I left home at 17, worked ten years in accountancy, hated it, but it paid the bills. Retrained and did another ten years working in mental health and absolutely loved it.

I have two dogs and a husband. I enjoy karaoke and love growing plants. I read books, hate coffee and intensely dislike clothes shopping. I love my family and friends and that's me. Ordinary. Unremarkable. Except –

Except.

By the age of 36 I had miscarried five pregnancies. One of those pregnancies was twins. I have lost six babies. I then had a total hysterectomy due to severe stage four endometriosis. They took my ovaries, too, so I went into full-blown menopause overnight at 34. I'll never know what it feels like to hold my children in my arms.

This story is profoundly personal and painful: savage, brutal agony in the deepest part of my soul. I'm writing it because I have to: because there is real danger that it will consume me if I don't. I'm going to be open and honest – I don't know any other way to do this. And if it helps someone wrestling with their own pain, their own trauma, their own lost babies, good. Better than good, because then this can be the legacy, the lasting value that I leave behind when the time comes.

It's a record of my long journey through a terrible time and it will be honest and heart-warming, a little bit funny, definitely a little bit sad, but most importantly I want to give you hope. I hope my book reassures you there is plenty of potential for a happy life, even though your life may not currently be as you might have planned it or wanted it to be.

One in four women will experience a miscarriage.

I think this book can tell you that whatever you have gone through and whatever you are facing, it is absolutely fine to be feeling whatever you are feeling right now. It will give you a heads up as to what you can expect in a life with no little ones at your side. Our situations and experiences may look similar, but everyone is different, and we deal with things in different ways.

We are the one in four, and you are not alone.

CHAPTER TWO
The One-Liner
2015

"Have you got kids?"

I'm at a summer barbeque, and the hand grenade has been thrown, and lies on the sunlit grass between us. Do I ignore it? Throw myself on it? Stuff it down this annoying, smug, professional mother's throat?

Sigh. If only. This is an inevitable question, whatever the gathering, it's become more frequently asked as childless time ticks on.

How do I respond? If I go for a simple "no", chances are it'll be followed up with passive-aggressive probing, peculiar facial expressions and questions like "oh, right, did you not want them, or…"

I'll take a large "OR…" to go, please.

The only real way to shut them up is to tell them the truth and I just don't want to. I'm exhausted and hurt, and oddly protective of my pain. It's mine, they can't have it, they haven't earned it. I have.

I think when I say the words out loud, I feel sort of winded by how horrible my journey has been. It literally sucks the breath out of me to go back and re live it.

I sit here staring at the screen struggling to see through the tears in my eyes, wondering how the heck I'm not dribbling and catatonic somewhere in a darkened room, stuffed full of medication. There are times when, for short spells I have been. Those times are an oddly peaceful memory. Hmmm.

Generally, I don't talk about it. Occasionally if I've had a few drinks, it comes out, but it's rare these days. I like to keep it squashed down deep inside so I can live my life relatively well without it bubbling at the surface constantly like a screaming kettle.

Sometimes people very kindly inform me that I ought to hurry up because that clock is ticking away.

It's not the clock, love, it's the hand grenade you threw.

I can see clearly that you think that your clock stopped ticking the moment you over filled your face with Botox, so, perhaps we oughtn't be so judgy hmm? Cockwomble.

People are so delightful.
I'm not unkind, but sometimes it's so sore, it causes a snap back of something hyper-attacking/defensive in my mind.

So, when I really can't avoid some kind of explanation, I try to keep it short and sweet. Look, I just wanted a normal life, I just wanted to come out to the BBQ like normal people do on a Saturday afternoon, why must I always be interrogated by all the stroller-pushers?

Thinking about it now, I think I keep it pretty much to a one-liner, just to change the subject as quickly as possible. Also, because I've just spotted where the wine cooler is, and I could do with a little glass of numb right about now.

"Have you got kids?"

Tick, tick, tick.

Maybe I'll just say I have a headache and head home.

I'm a nice person but it brings out some internal venom in me and my response in my head is nothing like what's coming out of my mouth.

Fortunately.

No, I haven't. Faff off Sandra, If I had kids,
they'd be here playing with all the other kids
wouldn't they, why are you asking? Please go
and step on a plug.

BOOM. No more grenade.

I hate her already.
"No, I wasn't well and had to have a
hysterectomy, but I'm much better now and it's
all ok."
This has the benefit of being mostly true. I try to
give a little smile with that one, just to promptly
quash any of their looks of pity and the
simultaneous head tilts, and to avoid those
wonderfully thoughtful soothing suggestions
about how I can adopt or foster. (Ah, can I?

Brilliant I wasn't aware! Cheers for that helpful
information!)
They couldn't win though.
If I hadn't had an invitation I'd have felt left out.
Also it's an entirely normal question. But it was
her manner.

The "It's all ok" on the end, somehow makes
people feel more comfortable about the whole
thing. I find people appear to almost feel guilty
about having their own children when they talk
to me (which actually makes me feel really sad).
I just like to get that line out of the way as
quickly as possible and move onto something
else. I can see it in their eyes. I reassure them
it's all ok, and I see the relief wash over them.
'Oh! She says it's all ok! Thank goodness!'

Yes, that's it Sandra, you can calm back down, Hun. Excuse me, you're standing between me and the drinks table, move it woman, I'm parched for a little glass of escape!

Because we're British, you see? The British don't like to talk about anything personal, anything uncomfortable, or anything which involves feelings or emotions. The stiff upper lip is still very much part of the English culture. So, I find it easier to use my one liner and then everybody's happy. Or it's swept back under the rug at the very least. Out of sight, out of mind and all that.

There is only one other time it comes out. It's different, I can be myself and I don't need to be armed with that one liner because it's generally when I'm sitting on the sofa with Adam in the evenings. There will be something on television, perhaps a film. Perhaps it's in the script that one of the characters is pregnant, and they excitedly attend their ultrasound, and the Ultrasound technician pops out and brings in a doctor. The doctor looks at the screen and then looks at the mother laid there with jelly on her tummy, and he tells her he's very sorry but there's no longer a heartbeat. That happened to me. Again, and again. The same crappy film, endlessly repeated.

Or perhaps a documentary, where a woman is telling her story about when she was pregnant, and she started to bleed, and she realised she was losing her baby.

That's when my really raw feelings come
because that happened to me too.

They come, these raw feelings, in the form of a
single silent tear. As my eyes sting and start to
fill, the single tear trickles down my cheek, onto
my chin, and drops onto my top, I quickly wipe
it away with my sleeve, and my husband
squeezes my hand or my leg to let me know
that its ok for me to be feeling feelings, and it's
ok to cry. But still I suck those other tears back
in, mostly because I'm terrified that if I let more
than one fall that they won't ever stop. Or I
might begin to wail, you know? When
something hurts you so profoundly in the
deepest parts of your soul and when you cry, it
isn't the cry of a human being. It comes out like
a wailing sound, like an injured animal or

something similar. To be honest when that happens it gives me a terrible emotion-hangover headache afterwards, and the sound I make frightens the dogs, so I suck those tears back up, and squash it all back down again. I nip out for a quick cigarette in the back garden (don't you dare judge me), think about something else and carry on with the evening. Under the rug, you see? We have huge rugs, we Brits, and massive brooms.

CHAPTER THREE
It's NOT your fault.

2019

I'd had terribly heavy, painful, and problematic periods since I started them at 11, but I was in my late twenties when I finally had my first laparoscopy. This is a surgical procedure where they make small incisions in the abdomen in my case, and they use a camera to do surgery via keyhole. They can look around and do certain further treatments while they are already inside, in some cases. It was then that the surgeon told me that I had Endometriosis. That, along with thyroid disease, was the possible cause of my difficulty in conceiving and subsequent losses. There are several stages of endometriosis, mine was stage 4. It had spread right down into my hip joint and grown down around the ligament. All around my bowel, it had spread onto both ovaries and bladder. I had a frozen pelvis. Usually your insides move quite freely, nice and silky, they move with you when you move. Mine don't. My uterus was stuck to my bowel. One of my ovaries had stuck to my uterus, and another section of my bowel was stuck to the other ovary. I was covered in this cruel and extremely painful condition. I knew from previous trips to hospital in my early twenties that I had had a large 10cm blood filled cyst on my ovary. The surgeon told me it had burst and left residue in my abdominal cavity some time ago. Also, there was another on my other ovary, which the surgeon had burst and cleared out during this procedure.

I found some relief in having a diagnosis.

To put it bluntly, when you can't seem to carry a baby longer than 14 weeks, and they keep dying inside you, you can't help but wonder if you have been doing something wrong. Self-blame is horrible. Not knowing, for so many years, why each of your babies doesn't survive, is really hard. So, for that specialist to tell me that it wasn't my fault, that I hadn't done anything wrong, that I wasn't to blame was a welcome conversation, although it didn't take away the pain from my losses. I'm not sure when that will go, or if it ever will. For now, I continue to carry that around.

I had eight surgeries in total over the next 4 years for endometriosis. Nine including the hysterectomy. It just kept growing back. The pain was unreal. I had adhesions everywhere in my abdomen. Adhesions are bands of scar tissue which can grow around the inside of the abdomen, or anywhere actually after trauma, infection, or surgery. They form like tight bands around the bowel for example, obstructing it and sometimes cutting off blood supply. Often people need surgery to remove parts of intestine which have died due to strangulation. It was unbelievably painful. I wouldn't wish it on anyone.

Apart from Julie, you'll hear about *her* later on.

I still have pain and adhesions from the last surgery, and it's an absolute nightmare sometimes. There are days which are bearable and manageable, others are just horrific. The level of physical pain can be really a lot to bear. Extremely hard to manage. It really depends which day you ask me. I could opt for another surgery to clear the adhesions, but by doing that, more surgery would cause yet more of this scarring to form. So, I choose to live with it the best way I can.

Surgical adhesions are debilitating, and when the surgeon says, "I'm afraid we've done everything that we can, it's about pain management now" and you have to find a way to manage, because that is your only option.

Any chronic or recurring illness like this is sad, and painful and life changing for people who live with it day to day. It can also be mortifying because the problematic areas which need to be checked are the parts we least want looking at with a magnifying glass, but needs must.

I vividly remember going for a colonoscopy. This is where they give you a sedative, but you're still awake in most cases, and they fill your intestines with air and slide a little camera on a tube into your rear orifice. This is the politest way I can describe it. British culture is still stuck in its ways with regards to what is acceptable to openly talk about, anything 'toilety' is taboo. Some of the tests you might have to go for aren't discussed in general and because of this you can have a very rude awakening when you turn up to an appointment. It's very much "Tut Tut! Oooh no dear we don't discuss these things, hush now, shush you don't want everybody to know!"

But how else are you going to find out? How can you prepare yourself for the things you might have to endure when no-one wants to talk about it?

How do you know what to really expect?

 I'm breaking taboos, so here's what happens, and I make absolutely no apologies for pre warning unsuspecting souls who could find themselves in the dark here.

The air is necessary to open up the inside of the colon, so they can take biopsies and have a look for any cause of pain. It doesn't take long; you can walk your groggy self out of the hospital after a couple of hours.

Think about it: the air has to go someplace, right?

Sooo... there I am, back in time. I need to share this experience *exactly* as it happened.

I am laid there half groggy, still on the gurney while the doctor is just typing the notes, and I feel a pain, I wince a little and the nurse offers to help me turn over in a sec once they're finished, so that I'm more comfortable. I agreed that would be lovely, I absolutely was not comfortable, and my mouth was beginning to feel like an old leather sandal, I was spitting feathers. I was ready to sit up a bit and take some sips of water. She tells me they're just removing the tube.

I should let you know, that to make it easier for the tube to go in, they smother it with half a gallon of KY Jelly, so it just slips right in. It also slips right out once they're done and as it did, I let out a relaxed sigh. This was quickly followed by a really, really long rumbling grumbling trump. "Oh no! I'm very sorry!" I don't know whether it was the effects of the sedative, but I was suddenly feeling emotional. I'd had enough of being prodded, poked and probed in every orifice by medics. I just wanted to go home to my dogs and my bed. I started to weep this really pathetic little cry.

Clearly wanting to comfort me, the nurse comes and takes my hand, explains that it's ok, everybody does it, the air has to go somewhere, and it happens every day. She reassures me that I don't need to be embarrassed and I start to settle down.

She hands me a tissue and helps me turn so that I'm more comfortable.
Listen, there's no other way to say it but what goes in must come out... and as she was close to my bottom area, getting the blanket sorted to cover me after she helped me turn, it

happened. I twisted slightly, she had half a hand under me, her face could not have been more than 8 inches from my rear end. Out it came. It started off as a high-pitched squeak, but it quickly evolved into the most enormous raspberry fart which must have lasted a whole 6 or 7 seconds. She shifted with whiplash speed, jolting her whole body back a foot, but it was too late. She had been too close for at least 2 seconds of the fart, which as it turned out, with all the KY, was a wet one. Not poopy or anything, because I'd had to drink a colon cleanser drink the day before. There was absolutely nothing in my bowels apart from gas and lube...(which they had put in there, just to be clear). Nevertheless, it must have been deeply unpleasant for her but I was no longer crying. I was laughing uncontrollably and the more I laughed the more I tensed my tummy muscles and the more air I farted out. It just kept coming. The more I tried to hold it in the more powerful it became, as I used all my might to squeeze my pelvic floor muscles to prevent this from continuing, to try to hold it inside, the worse it got. The beautiful angel said not to worry about it, handed me some paper tissues, (to wipe the moist area) and she excused herself and went, presumably for a shower, a breath of fresher air and to question her life and career choices. Once she left the room, I turned fully on my side and just allowed it to happen. It escaped like a giant thunderclap, then my buttocks gave a round of applause and I was empty. Oh, such sweet relief, if I were religious,

I might have praised Jesus at that moment for breaking up the agony. Every time I remember this moment in my life. It has me howling with laughter.

I hope they gave her the rest of the day off; she deserved it.

Earlier that year, in the summertime, I met a new work colleague, Maggie. I'm from England but my husband Adam and I moved to the Channel Islands in January 2017. I met Maggie at the induction for my job. She was a psychiatric nurse from the UK, and I'm a psychiatric Support worker. I realised she didn't know anyone and wasn't familiar with where anything on the island was. She had moved over by herself. It was different for Adam and me when we moved here because we had each other. So, I gave her my number in case she needed anything.

The following Saturday came a glorious sunny afternoon and I had been potting some plants out in the back yard. She sent me a message asking where she could buy cushion covers, and I asked what she was doing for the rest of the day. I invited her over to our house and we sat in the back garden with a glass of wine. By glass, of course I mean bottle. She asked about children, and I gave my one liner. But then she asked whether I had tried to have children before I became unwell, and I wasn't prepared. I couldn't one-line myself out of that one. So, I talked briefly about my first marriage, and how I had tried hard, been pregnant several times but it hadn't worked out.

Every word that left my mouth stabbed me inside my aching heart, as I briefly relayed the previous decade or so in around five lines, and then I shut it down again. She seemed almost distracted by the fact I wasn't more emotional. She asked how I coped. How did I manage to come through that? How do I hold it together so well? My response was that If I were emotional, I'd break, I told her that I cope because I don't have any other choice, and I hold it together because I have to. It's true, that nobody really knows their strength until being strong is the only option they have left.

Then, joy of joys, as I closed off, she opened up.

She told me her son had had a baby boy who had died only a few days after being born. It was then that I saw in her eyes that she understood my pain. She understood the complexity of this vastly unspoken subject, and I somehow felt warmer and less alone knowing she could relate.

It's like a silent club in my experience. You can expect that quite often if you meet someone who has had first-hand experience of this kind of crushing loss, that when you open up to them about what happened to you, they might also open up and feel able to speak more freely, than they may have done in the company of someone who has no knowledge of it.

In my experience if you cross paths with someone this way, and you're both able to chat without prejudice, the reward is a very special warm feeling – almost like a 'belonging' if you will. There are many women who will never talk about their loss or losses, and that's absolutely ok, we each deal whichever ways we can. All that matters is what works for you.

I have discovered along my own path in life, that I'm actually a little bit of both. I want the opportunity to talk freely when I want to about this dark and lonesome subject. But it's like a shared "knowing" and I get great benefit from this at times. It's as if when you meet someone else who "knows", you aren't so alone with it. Strength in numbers if you understand my drift?

I'm also a woman who goes for months without talking about it. We are like flowers... we might open, then reseal.

Maggie left after only 4 months, but I was blessed to have met her.

Several silent tears slipped from my eyes that afternoon, and I didn't have to hide a single one.

CHAPTER FOUR
Ivory Sofa
2020

There are certain times that I find really difficult, even now, many many years on from my last miscarriage. I noticed that as the years passed, I always feel emotionally battered at the start of a new school year, and this is partly down to FacebookTwitterInstaTikTok, as you'll see.

This is the flip side of how I have felt.

As you come through my journey with me, you'll notice my tone and outlook changes often and by now you'll hopefully start to understand what I mean, when I say expect the unexpected. This journey is chaotic emotionally. Life changes, feelings change, but sometimes those feelings can sit stagnant and fragmented deep in the heart. This may leave you feeling feelings that you don't understand, and they can manifest in unexpected ways. This doesn't mean you are a bad person. It's part of a process. I certainly had at least a year where I held anger, bitterness and absolute choking envy of anyone who had what I so desperately wanted.

Every chapter here has a feeling, and the feelings change because this is exactly what happens in real life. It's so easy to take the pain deep inside and hold it there.

During these times there's nothing quite like logging in and seeing 15,793 posts related to the first day of school and photos of their little progeny in their uniforms stood by the fireplace/front door. I just find it profoundly painful. The realms of emotions are like a tirade of paintballs all being directed at you by 100, all at once at a point-blank range. Except real paintballs leave bruises and a visible array of paint splattered all over you.

The pain we endure, you cannot see.

Another level of internal conflict is when a baby is born. I am always genuinely happy for friends when they have babies, and I truly mean that. But when they start photographing the hapless infant with a card that says, "I am one day old today!" I'm trying hard not to sound bitter, because the truth is if I had children myself, I would probably do this too. But it hurts.

And truthfully that isn't me, to feel conflicted this way. Not one little bit. My personality generally is that of a butterfly (I've been told). Non offensive, just does her own thing, helps people and charities whenever she can, and is known for her empathy.

But there's an unseen elephant waiting around every corner.

There have been times where the pain within myself, has been heavier than my happiness for others. One or two of these photos or cards is fine, I don't object. But when it's never ending, I have to mute people. It's a constant bombardment like a punch in the face because it then goes on to another photo the next day with a card "I am two days old today!" Then the third day, and fourth, and fifth, it just goes on and on, and it just pretty much continues until they're 21 years 4 months 6 days and 17 hours old and it turns out they never did grow into that enormous head they were born with, which is unfortunate.

Do you see what I mean? Who had I become thinking thoughts like that? Where did my kindness go?

This bitterness fades, you'll be relieved to hear, as the years passed.

Phew.

At the time, when the rawness was really red raw, I was of the opinion that it's lovely that they're all so adorable and cute and squishy, but when did it become obligatory to photograph your child every 22 seconds and then share it with the metaverse? Is it just me?

The best way I can word what living with this kind of bereavement is like, is absolutely *jarring*. You notice the loss and emptiness literally everywhere you go. If it's a more recent loss, you can expect to suddenly notice that every woman you meet from that point appears to be pregnant. All at once, there seem to be more children wherever you go. So when an every day thing like popping onto Facebook to wish your cousin a quick good luck for a job interview that morning, suddenly becomes an entire day consisting of calling in sick and lying to your boss (because feeling sad about this 2 months after it happened isn't a good enough reason apparently to not go into work) drawing the living room curtains, building yourself a fort, getting in it and sobbing your agonized heart out, all because you took a second out of your morning, and that bloody elephant came and trampled you.

Can we just go back to having a birthday once a year? Like normal people? Please? You can hear that I'm saying that through gritted teeth, can't you?
Thank god for Mark Zuckerberg and the mute button.

I sound really bitter I know, but honestly, I'm not. It makes me happy to see other people happy.

It's just that my pain is heavy, like weight that no diet in the world is ever going to shift. Making cutting comments in my head sometimes helps to take the edge off the pain.

Photos aren't special anymore, the smartphone put an end to that: anyone born before the nineties will have watched the change with a certain amount of bemusement, as I did.

I think it's because people used to take photos of meaningful milestones and put them in a little album and bring that album out when their child brought home a girlfriend/boyfriend. It would be cute and funny, and end up in a box in the attic. Now, everybody is swamped with other people's baby photos, and it's not just me who feels this way. I have friends **with** children who complain that they come on to social media to have a break from their kids, only to get spammed with photo after photo of other people's clogging up their newsfeed.

Only occasionally it stings me that I don't have that. I'll never iron their gym kit, comb their hair, walk them to school, or read bedtime stories.

I just want to flip the coin for a minute.

This will be difficult for me to explain, and you might think I'm awful for how I feel, but it is how it is, and I promised you, and myself, that I'd be honest with you.

As the years have gone on, I'm 50/50 torn, and I feel bad about the way I feel. I wanted children. I tried hard to have them. I was lost and devastated each time one of my babies left me. I am left with all of those feelings, and they Never.Go.Away. Never.

Now, my wants and needs have changed. I'm very happily married to my second husband, I'm older, I'm probably wiser, I'm definitely more comfortable with myself and I'm more understanding of how the world works, if occasionally less patient with it. I understand now that sometimes things happen, or don't happen, without explanation. Life, as has been observed, can just be a bitch.

In my healing journey this realisation was a pinnacle point. As soon as I came to accept it, my daily life didn't hurt quite so much. Sometimes there just is no rhyme or reason for things. I used to question, 'why me?' 'Why has this happened to me?' but actually, why not? Sad things happen to people all the time. So why not me?

I'm more accepting in general as I've got older, that some things just aren't meant to be. If I were 29 years old, divorced, with five children would I have met my second husband? Would I have the love and happiness in my marriage today if I had had all of my children around me? If they were with me, I'd still be tied to my ex-husband and would have to see him every other weekend when he picked them up. If I had my children, I'd be very busy with laundry, ironing, packed lunches, after school clubs and I probably wouldn't have time to even take a bath in peace, let alone have a romantic life.

If I had my children, I'd love them unconditionally. But I don't have them. I have so much love for my husband, we love each other so much and dote on each other and I honestly don't know if there's room in our relationship for babies or small children (and the dogs would probably agree). If we had young kids, we wouldn't be able to swan off on holiday when the fancy takes us, he wouldn't have the freedom to say "get dressed honey, I'm taking you out for dinner" - we'd have to call a sitter, we could never be spontaneous again. We'd be getting up six times a night for feeds and changes. We'd have no money because Christmas and school uniforms alone would bankrupt us. I'd be scrubbing yoghurt out of the carpets every other day, and googling tips on how to remove crayon from the walls. I wouldn't have the life I have now. I have friends who are exhausted 24/7. Seriously, they struggle so much and find things so hard. Some remind me how lucky I am to be able to go on holiday, just the two of us. It's a strange position I'm in actually, and I think to some of my friends it has been beneficial to have a friend who doesn't have children. A couple have told me about their parenting struggles and they openly say," I can tell you because you haven't got kids so you won't judge me" Or," I feel like I can tell you, If I told so and so she would tell all the other mums and they'd be judgmental". I'm told by one of my most favourite people in the world, that female friends who don't have children are the cornerstones of her sanity. It takes a village. I hadn't actually thought of myself that way before.

So, if I had my life over again, would I choose to try and try and try for children, or would I just accept what is, and enjoy my life as it was obviously intended to be for me? It's a good question. I don't know, is the answer. My thoughts on this change daily. As I've matured, I am drawn to a peaceful quiet and serene type of life. I don't know whether that's because this is who I am as a person, or whether I have just learned to love my life because I know this is the way it will be without little ones, possibly a bit of both. If I hadn't had to have a hysterectomy and I found out I was pregnant today, would I be overjoyed? Actually, you know what? I don't think I would. I don't relish the idea of my little darlings smearing chocolate handprints on the wallpaper, and I enjoy having an ivory sofa. At age 26 yes absolutely, I wanted at least three! But at thirty-six, and I don't know if it's all the drama so far, but I'm a little more tired. So maybe I was just never meant to be a mother. Still feels odd to write that, though.

Once you know that you'll never be expecting, you can expect to feel a mixture of emotions, and have back and forth battles with yourself about a life with children, and a life without. Feelings of guilt about enjoying a quiet life without little ones, whilst also still feeling devastation at the loss of the hope and promise of the lives of the ones you held in your stomach. Swings and roundabouts. Or not.

And my goodness, it can be confusing at times.

CHAPTER FIVE
Annus Horriblius: the front end
2010

This was definitely the worst year of my adult life, so much so that I've split it into two chapters. Feel free to have a break and a cuppa in the middle. You could even join me in a cocktail. I promise not to do a 'Julie revenge move'. More of that later!

In January 2010, I found out I was pregnant with twins. I can't tell you how excited I was. But, almost immediately I started bleeding and was told at the hospital that I had lost one of my twins. It was touch and go with the second one. I was going daily to hospital to have blood work done to make sure my pregnancy hormones were increasing properly. Each day I didn't know if the second twin would survive. But I was hopeful, and as the weeks went by my pregnancy hormones increased and I was more positive.

I went another month before the Doctor confirmed that my second twin had also passed away. That was the longest I ever carried a child. I had been pregnant for 14 weeks and 2 days when I went home to allow my body to expel my 'pregnancy remains' as they so delightfully worded it.

March was my birthday. I planned a big night out with about thirty friends. Some were coming from all over the UK, so I had twelve staying at my house that night. We'd been out and had the most amazing time. It was exactly what I needed after the last few months. When we got back to my house, I went upstairs to grab extra blankets. My friend Julie lived locally but had asked could she also stay, because she was struggling to get a taxi. I said of course, and it was for her that I had gone to get the extra blanket.

As I came back down the stairs, I felt something.

My stomach flip flopped, I opened the door and their faces pulled away from each other in less than a fraction of a second. The room was dimly lit but I saw them. I turned the light on, and everything looked normal. I'd had a few drinks, so I sort of shrugged it off, I must have been mistaken. Although I wouldn't have put it past Nick, I knew Julie wouldn't do that to me. The house fell into a mixture of snoring and quiet, as I lay there telling myself I was being silly, and my eyes were playing tricks. My hormones were probably still settling down. I was oversensitive. She definitely would never do that to me. Would she?

Julie was the friend I'd met about a year before, She's the friend who came to my house and curled on the bed and held me while I sobbed on the day of our most recent baby loss. She texted me every day, she brought flowers, she brought fruit and chocolate, she took me out for lunch.

Julie wouldn't do that to me.

No, definitely not.

The next morning, I cooked breakfast for the masses of hungover souls who had travelled from far and wide to be with me on my special evening. The least I could do was rustle up something greasy to help settle their stomachs, which had been heavily abused by cocktails and shots the night before. Everything was normal, some had left but ten or so people sat around chatting and munching bacon sandwiches, gradually starting to depart one by one to return to their own beds to sleep the rest off. It was all totally normal, except it wasn't.

I had a feeling; I couldn't shake it. I didn't want to believe what I thought I'd seen. So, after everyone left, I asked him outright.

"Did something happen with you and Julie last night? I saw something when I opened the door."

He told me they had kissed. That she had leaned in and kissed him, and he had kissed her back, he told me it was a moment of weakness and he told me he was sorry. I went to bed to hide from my life, and while I was there he said he was sorry again. Publicly. On social media. I didn't see it for 6 hours, and by then everyone, including my family knew what he'd done. It was in the open. A trusted friend had cheated on me with my husband. Her betrayal hurt me just as much as useless Nick's.

I was utterly crushed and I couldn't hide. I cut Julie out of my life and watched Nick like a hawk.

A few weeks later, I was out celebrating a friend's birthday and Julie came over to me. Maybe she wanted to make amends but for me there was no going back. She put her hand on my waist and told me I looked great. I wanted to say "Yes, bitch! I've been on the Betrayal Diet! It melts the pounds away!" Instead, I let my body do the talking. I jerked backwards, raised my drinking arm and chucked my newly purchased, bright red cocktail over her white dress. Woo Woo really does make a splash! Turns out that revenge is a dish best served cold, with ice and an umbrella.

The Woo Woo Revenge helped me gain some control over my life but this horrible year hadn't finished with me yet.

A couple of months later, my best friend Lucy took her own life. I was bereft, empty, lost. She had been my closest friend for six long years. She had been by my side through my increasingly bad marriage and had seen me through many difficult times. And I, I hope, had done the same for her. She talked to me for hours through so many heartaches of losses when he hadn't. She had been my source of adventure, fun and happiness through some of my darkest times, and suddenly she was gone. The memory from that morning is fresh, as if it were yesterday. It was around 10.30am and I was washing my hair in the shower. I heard the phone ring, which was unusual – normally people call the mobile rather than the house phone. I heard him shout out that he had it. So I slowed my pace, wrapping my hair in the towel, twisting, flipping the head back, bit of moisturiser on the face and out onto the landing I came, still rubbing it in.

"Who was that?" I asked.

"Chloe, it's Lucy…"

His face was very serious.

"...she hung herself last night."

Now, I have to explain that out of the 6 years Lucy and I had been close friends, the last two of those were a very difficult time for her, mental health wise, and so it wasn't actually too unusual when I got a call in the night/early hours to say, Lucy is in hospital, she cut her wrists/overdosed etc.

Usually at this point I'd find out which ward, I'd throw my trainers on and bolt up to the A&E department, about ten minutes run from my home.

"Oh god, OK, where is she, I'll just dry my hair real quick."

He shook his head.

I blinked.

No.

"Where is she?"

"Chloe, she died. I'm sorry."

No.

NO.

"Who called?"

"Her sister."

I blinked again.

NO.

"You've got it wrong, I'll call her. You must have misunderstood."

No. No. No.

No. No.

Please, please, *please* fucking *no*.

My fingers visibly shaking I found the name on the phone, I pressed, it was answered immediately.

'Hey, Nick just said…'

"She's gone."

"What? What do you mean she's gone?"

"She died last night. Around half nine. She had gone up for a bath and she used the tie from her dressing gown. She's dead."

No.

I said, "hold on… I'll call you back in two."

I hung up.

I did not call her back in two.

I stood there, hair in towel and phone in hand, until it slipped to the floor and bounced, landing screen up, showing the photo of us on my wallpaper picture. My vision blurred, I ran ice cold, I wanted to vomit.

My legs buckled.

My body leaned into the wall and I slid all the way down.

I remember being really low down on the floor. I wanted it to just take me, swallow me, stop the air around me from stinging.

A million knives throughout the deepest depths of my soul.

Everything echoed, I could hear my heartbeat and all my pulses at the same time.

She promised she'd never leave me.

But she did.

She's dead.

Nobody could intervene this time. She had successfully ended her life.

My world stopped turning.

Then, the sound came. It wasn't human, it wasn't me, it wasn't my voice. It came from me, but I didn't recognise this as a sound of mine.

Life would never be the same again.

And it wasn't... It was never the same.

The losses I'd had, followed by the loss of her?

Nope.

I just absolutely *couldn't* cope.

Many years on I'm doing much better. I cope better, and this is due in large part to a treatment called EMDR. This is a fascinating treatment. It helps to 'dim' traumatic experience so you can find a way to live with it. I didn't think it would work, but I'd tried everything else. But bit by bit over 3 years I tackled my issues with a couple of specialists. I didn't recognize it at the time but the work they did with me changed my life.

I knew that Lucy had struggled with her mental health, and now, many years later, I understand that she did it because her pain was unbearable.

She didn't do it to leave *me*, abandon *me*, hurt *me*, or punish me. She did it because her agony had been too much for too long.

For several years after she passed away, I saw it very differently. I had lost her. She had left me. I took it extremely personally. They say in your darkest moments of life, even your shadow leaves you. She was my shadow, and she had left me.

Lucy was amazing. I didn't have another friend like her, until I met Beth.

Beth has now been my best and closest friend of more than a decade, she has two beautiful boys and I love them. My life is happier for having her in it and it's a beautifully balanced friendship. I can't imagine life without her, and that's a great thing.

I don't know about you, but I've had enough of the sad stuff. Let's have a giggle about funny dribble!

I had to go for a check up scan at the hospital because my GP thought I may have a blood clot in my leg. I toddled off and sat and waited patiently. An hour later a student nurse came and took me to the triage room, where she looked at my leg then sent me back to the waiting room while she disappeared to get a tape measure. I sat, staring at the posters on the walls and then I noticed a young man, only around 18 or so. He got up and grabbed a magazine from the pile on the table. I watched in absolute horror as he sat back down and proceeded to lick his thumb... Flick the page... Lick his thumb again... Flick the next page.

I studied human physiology and psychology and I know that this is normal behavior for a lot of people. That is the problem.

The student nurse came back and measured my leg with the tape measure but I was unable to take my eyes off the finger licking car crash. He's going to get sick. All the sick people come here and lick their thumbs and flick that page, on that exact magazine and put the thumb back in their mouth like he's doing right now. I feel sick thinking about the bacterial microbes and his saliva... And the previous ones. I must have had my mouth gaping in horror because the nurse told me one calf yes, in fact was 3cm bigger than the other one and as I looked down at her a long string of my own saliva landed on her top.

She did not notice. I pondered whether I should tell her because you know, health and safety, germs, cross contamination but I didn't know how to word what had happened. So I just pretended it hadn't happened at all.

I bet that young lad got sick though.

Remember I said the year hadn't finished with me yet?
In June of 2010, I found out Nick was playing away again.

And of course, I knew. I knew he was seeing someone and lying about where he'd been because one day he went to visit his dad but was an hour and a half late coming back. I phoned his dad to ask what time he'd left, concerned maybe he had car trouble and his phone had died on a dark country lane. Or maybe, because I'd lost so much already that year, I was concerned he'd had an accident. So, I was worried.

But his dad told me Nick hadn't visited that day. When Nick returned home, He came through to the lounge and said hello, and proceeded to tell me that his dad sent his love to me. I knew then. I sat and pondered for a couple of hours. Most wives would have been absolutely devastated at the mere suspicion that their husbands were sneaking around but to be honest I was used to it. It had happened at least three times (that I know of for certain) in the years we had been together, but this time was different. So much had happened this year, I was struggling, and I was questioning very seriously how my life was going.

As a result, I knew that I was *not* content to turn the other cheek and wait for this one to run its course. I confronted him.

I was very calm, I went into the little room where he was playing on his Xbox.
"I need to have a talk with you."
As usual he didn't look up from the screen.

"I know you're seeing someone; I know that you lied about seeing your dad that day. I spoke to your dad. Tell me the truth this time."

He paused the computer game and went pale. I knew it was serious because that one time I slipped on the stairs, he hadn't even paused his game to come and check on me.

He looked at the floor, the room silent, and his controller still in his hands.

"I've been seeing someone."

"Yes, I know."

"She's pregnant."

All the bones in my body dissolved instantly and I turned to jelly. I stood there for a full minute as all the blood drained to my feet. I felt sick. I couldn't breathe. My life, which had already fallen apart in those previous few months, now changed forever. This was a game changer. There was no coming back. Nick had created a new life, with someone other than me, his wife. I was the one he promised to love through thick and thin but someone else had been able to give him the one thing I couldn't. I'd tried so hard to give him a baby in the ten years we'd been together. Now he had been sneaking around and got some bit of fluff up the duff.

My god, this hurt like I'd been stabbed.

I stood silent while he looked at me for my reaction. I think he thought I might do something extreme. Like scream or start slapping him.

It was a split-second decision, and I knew it would be huge. But things had already gone to shit, my life was looking like a dozen dropped quiches at this point. Sometimes you need to really hit rock bottom so you can rebuild.

This was it. I was quiet and calm. I didn't shout or cry. I didn't have any tears left for him, and I didn't have the energy. I was already broken. A few tiny words left my mouth. I told him there was no coming back from this, that I wanted a divorce. That if he wanted to pack a few things up right then and move in with her, that that was ok.

He wasn't sure what he wanted. I told him he would have to be gone by the end of the month. He nodded, told me he was sorry, and I silently left the room. Within a couple of minutes, the computer game was back on, and I knew I had made the right decision.

In June, we split up. In early July Nick moved out. I had lost my babies, my best friend, and my husband within 6 months. I was alone. Truly alone. I was utterly lost.

I couldn't cope, and I simply stopped eating: in the next eleven months, ten stones in weight fell from my once squishy body. It wasn't about being overweight in the beginning. It was because I was so very truly heartbroken. Lost amongst the many avenues of grief and change, I drowned in emotion. I was, in some really fundamental way, *broken*. My throat simply closed up, I physically couldn't swallow food so I just stopped. In those eleven months I went from 246lbs to 102lbs. At 5 feet nine inches tall, I was emaciated and diagnosed with Anorexia Nervosa. That was a whole other battle and it's not really relevant here, so I'm leaving that topic well alone, safe to say that I eventually I did emerge, at least functional again.

You can expect that one grief or loss, ties in with another. Every funeral I go to I'm reminded of the ones before. And all funerals remind me of my silent losses.

Every time I pass a baby clothing store, I'm reminded. Each time a friend has a child, I'm reminded. I can't watch certain films and because I ate a certain food on one of the days I had a loss, I can no longer eat that food, because the taste takes me back to a terrible day.

If I'm 100% truthful, I decided to leave my hometown and not return, partly because I wanted to live in a warmer place, but it was predominantly because those damned elephants were lurking everywhere. All the streets I'd walked down, restaurants I'd visited, parks I'd gone to, places I had to go for food shopping, at every single corner, the elephants loomed. A memory, where I'd been for lunch with Lucy, the park I would have taken my children to, the doctor's surgery I had attended so many times, the pharmacy I'd bought tests from, the place I'd married Nick. Just constant reminders everywhere of people I'd once loved so dearly, and lost so cruelly. I couldn't take it. Grief manifests in so many ways.

CHAPTER SIX
An(n)us Horribilis: the rear-end.

In September, Jamie asked me out on a date. He was the young guy I was buying weed off. It helped me with eating a little bit, it helped me sleep a little bit, and it helped me numb my internal emotional agony a lot. So, by this point I had started smoking it every day. (I told you I'd be honest)

He was the first person to ask me out for a long time and I had been stuck indoors with my thoughts for far too long. So, I said yes. Why the hell not?

This is why not: that date was the beginning of a very unhealthy, inconsistent, and unstable off and on relationship. We lived together as a couple when we were an item and house shared when we weren't. By this point in the year, I'll admit that I was desperate to be loved. I'd been rejected by my babies, abandoned by my best friend, and my marriage had ended. So naturally I became one of those women who didn't eat any food and allowed their fellas to treat them however they liked, and I didn't complain too much, because being with someone who was a shit boyfriend was better than being completely alone with these feelings... right? Yes, I got together with the drug dealer. Whoop-de-do. Like I said, very unhealthy.

You can expect to not feel great about yourself after baby loss. While you're vulnerable you need to protect yourself wherever you can.

The only constant while I was with Jamie was his son.

Ben had just turned three when I first met him, and honestly, he was so beautiful. Just before we got together properly, Jamie phoned me one evening in a panic, asking if I could come to his place and babysit. He said he had to go out but only for half an hour. I agreed. It was 9pm and pitch-black outside. I threw on my trainers and toddled down the same old long road and went up to the third floor to his tiny bedsit.

He pointed out the pull ups, wipes, sippy cups and said he wouldn't be long.

He kissed me at the door and left.

I sat with Ben for 4 hours that night, he slept angelically the entire time, never stirred.

I think I already realised I was a mug with regards to Jamie, but it was nice to be kissed, It felt like I hadn't been properly kissed for years, and I was so lost, so lonely and in so much pain. I'd been so heavily rejected by everything and anything I'd loved recently, and this little boy filled my heart with simple joy. A feeling I had been deeply lacking since I can remember.

His beautiful long eyelashes and pristine unblemished pure skin, his quiet little snorkels and peaceful sighs while he dreamt.
I fell absolutely in love with this little boy.

I watched him grow over the next couple of years, while he started school and had his birthday parties at his mum's house. We'd attend and be there like one whole big family. We got on well and I think she felt reassured that I cared very much about Ben and his well-being.

It was like being a stepmum but without the close link with the dad. It was kind of bizarre actually because Jamie and I were off and on but still always sharing a home. Two homes actually. I rented him a room after my separation but once we became a proper item, we got a house big enough for Ben to have his own room. Jamie and I had separate rooms with our own beds and TV etc but we were very much together and each night always shared a bed in one or others room.

We were weekend parents, co-parenting with Bens actual parents and it was strange, not the norm, but it worked. Ben was always looked after at weekends, properly fed and clean and cuddled and played with, with his toys and games. I absolutely adored him with all of my heart. Genuinely. To leave Jamie was incredibly sore, because I wasn't really leaving him, I was leaving this beautiful little boy, who had mistakenly called me "mummy" a few times when I was cooking his tea. I knew once I packed up and left, that I'd probably never see Ben again.

Before it ended, it all fitted like a jigsaw, despite the situation with Jamie being very unstable. In its own way it was...kind of wonderful, amazing, eye opening. But also, unpleasant, and emotional agony.

During the splits we'd still live in the same house and we'd be like very normal all weekend. Ben would be picked up at 6pm on a Sunday night. We'd kiss him goodbye, chat with his mum and wave them off in their car. Jamie would then say. "I got a few things to do" and he'd go out.

A few times he'd be back home within an hour, polish his room, hoover, spray air freshener, and then some random young girl would turn up at the door, I'd open it and she'd be there all in her push up bra and low cut top, loads of make-up and she'd be like "Hiya, is Jamie in?" And I'd show these little tramps in, in their ridiculous eyelashes, looking like painted horses and wave them up to his room.

What the actual???????

Anyway, I think that covers a bit of ground on the topic of Ben, and my love and adoration for him. And also, my heartbreak at losing my marriage, to be scooped up by this man Jamie, promised the earth, and steadily trampled to rock bottom whilst I was already down in the gutter.

What can you expect when you'll never ever be expecting?

You can expect to be so horribly broken that you drop your standards to absolutely below par, and you can expect that amongst your own agony, you'll find unexpected moments of joy. Absolute and total pure joy spending time with, becoming besotted with and playing pretend mama with someone else's baby.
I can also tell you, there have been points in time when I've felt as follows....

- It's not real.
- You aren't permanent.
- They won't even remember you.
- This won't last.

- It cannot go on forever, and when it ends...
- Expect it to hurt.
- Very Much.

That inner voice can be so hurtful can't it? It did hurt like hell though.

CHAPTER SEVEN
The nine lives

2023

Well, my Darlings, this is definitely trickier to write than I expected. It's been four years since I started writing about the heartache I've been carrying.

During that time everything has changed: I went on holiday with my husband and contracted Typhoid fever and almost died; there was the worldwide Covid-19 pandemic; and we emigrated to live a self-sufficient off grid life in the Spanish wilderness to grow our own food in the countryside. As you do.

Oh yes, and last year, I turned 39. And had a stroke.

Let's cover this in fits and bursts, I think. Although it's been such a genuinely horrific time, it was a turning point for me. I actually had two strokes, two months apart.
As a result of that first stroke, medics saw me here in Spain. They found a problem with my blood, which turned out to be a rare and nasty blood clotting disorder and because of it, I'll need treatment forever.
It's called Antiphospholipid Syndrome, otherwise known as Hughes Syndrome after Professor Graham Hughes, who discovered this illness in the year I was born, 1983.

I'm 40 now and by having this diagnosis I finally have answers to questions that have haunted me.

I never did do anything wrong to make my babies leave me.

100% it wasn't my fault.

Two prominent symptoms for this illness are migraine and recurrent pregnancy loss. Around 1 in 2000 people are diagnosed, however the actual number is closer to 1 in 500 with it being rarely tested for.

APS is an autoimmune disorder, and many people can have the antibodies for it, yet never have a clot and never have any issues, but there are some people, like me, who struggle greatly with it.

Looking back over my medical history the diagnosis explains much of it.

At age 21 I had a pulmonary embolism, a large blood clot in my lung. They were never sure what caused it and I was in hospital for 8 days. On my first day on the ward, I shuffled off the bed and started wandering over to the toilet, and the nurse came running, this look of absolute panic on her face. She stopped me in my tracks, told me to just stand still. Then she called for the doctor who explained to me that if I got up and walked around, the clot could

shoot to my heart or brain and kill me.

She wheeled me back to the bed in a

wheelchair. I was twenty-one, I hadn't really,

properly thought about myself and death so

closely together before.

All my miscarriages are now thought to have

been thrombosis related, as no other cause was

conclusively found.

Clots form between the mother and the baby, in

the placenta, in the umbilicus, anywhere

actually. It's not just in the big veins and

arteries, anywhere that blood flows within my

body, blood can clot.

A couple of years ago I had a pain in my leg for 4 days. I went to my GP and because I'd had a clot in my lung previously, he sent me off to the emergency room for scans just to be safe, and there it was.

A deep vein thrombosis, or DVT for short.

They suspected that I might have APS at that point. I was referred to a hematologist, she did some blood work, they came back positive. To be clinically diagnosed, my history and this result was enough but the normal procedure was to have the test repeated 12 weeks apart. She explained to me about APS and wanted to put me on warfarin. I declined the second test and the medication at that point, but hear me out as to why.

For the previous 6 years we had been saving. Like squirrels, saving every penny because we'd realised early on that our dream was to leave the UK and go to the warmth and sunshine of a rural Spanish village. Real Spanish life.

Finally we were in a position to make the move and we stepped into the world of nature, self-sufficiency, and organic farming. We bought our 20-acre farm in Spain and were due to begin the 26-hour drive through Europe in less than a month. It would take at least a month to get the dose of warfarin right and then it would all have to change when I got to Spain as the climate and food etc. all change the level of medicine needed. It's a medication which needs very close monitoring, daily in the beginning, then weekly I'd have to have blood taken for testing.

So, I promised her for the next month that I'd go onto aspirin daily and that once I arrived in Spain, I'd get a doctor and a specialist. However, with Brexit happening in England, it wasn't so straightforward.

I couldn't access the doctor regarding an existing health condition. If there was an emergency that was different. But until my Spanish residency came through I wasn't medicated for the APS.

For a year I plodded on as best as I could managing on aspirin.

I got sicker and sicker, more tired, and physically weak. More and more little clots formed in my hands, legs, feet. We could see weird rashes forming where tiny blood vessels had clotted and burst. I was not a picture of health on the outside and I was fearful of the state of my insides. All the weight I gained since my recovery from anorexia fell off, I was a rake again. I lost 100lbs that year.

I waited so patiently for my residency papers; it was just so agonisingly slow. I carried on chipping away into our beautiful new life, farming the land, creating a home, growing flowers from seeds, preserving sauces and fruit, and collecting firewood from the forest.

As I write this chapter I still live here, with my husband Adam on our little farm in the mountains.

On September 5th, 2022, everything changed, and at the time we had no idea just how much. I'd been harvesting the grapes that morning. I had a niggly chest cramp ever since I woke up. The previous day I'd been informed my mother was terminal with cancer, so I'd put it down to stress.

It continued into the next day, I could barely catch my breath. I told Adam to take me to hospital.

He put me in the car and off we dashed, an hour's drive through the mountains to the closest emergency department.

I was laid out on the gurney with all these medical people around, doing heart traces and blood pressure and all the machines beeping like the old-style internet dial up, and it happened.

It's hard to describe. I realised I'd slipped down the bed. I tried to push myself back up and couldn't use my leg or my arm, I was numb on one side.

I looked at Adam to tell him that I felt funny, but nothing came out. It was so bizarre, why wasn't my mouth working? A blurb of babble. A noise.

I saw his face and then I felt panicked. He told the nurse something was wrong, and then they all came. A dozen people maybe. They whipped me into the brain scanner so fast. That was the point that I started losing full concept of time. A blood clot was moving through my brain, interrupting the blood supply, starving my brain of oxygen. This type of brain interruption is known as a stroke. It lasted around 5 minutes, the medical report says, and for all of that time I was unable to speak. I lost the power of communication. What if I could never speak again? Would those closest to me know my wishes? Did they know me well enough to know that I prefer apple juice to orange? I do have recollection of bits, but some details are missing. My brain was swollen for several weeks afterwards. I had problems with balance, walking, talking, dressing etc. At that point in my life, everything was almost impossibly hard. For months afterwards it was just all so extremely difficult. Physically and emotionally soul destroying. I couldn't work or tend my little farm. I couldn't do basic things like walk with a watering can. I sat for week after week, month after month watching all my hard work become grown over, brown, dried up and neglected. My husband did absolutely all he could to take care of me while I was unwell, he also had to do all the things I couldn't do, but there just were not enough hours in the day for him to keep the crops alive too: that in itself is a full time job.

What happened to me that day hurt my heart. It flicked something emotionally inside me. I felt so many outrageous feelings which drifted from absolute self-pity for myself that I couldn't put my own socks on if my feet got cold, but also a weird mixture of feelings of second chances, new hope, and seeing the world a different way.

I was still alive, when I could very easily have died. I was so grateful.

As soon as I was well enough, I voice recorded little adventure stories about my two dogs and their antics on our farm. I sat each day resting, but also watching. Once I was well enough, I wrote the stories down. When that was too hard, I drew the pictures for my children's stories. On really tricky days, I did the colouring-in. Every day I tried to do what I could. To *keep going.* I found real unexpected enjoyment from it.

The gratitude was unreal. I was noticing beautiful things like the sweet scent of the almond blossom on the trees. The birds glided that little bit more majestically, and Adam, if it's at all possible, looked that little bit more handsome to me.

After the experience of losing my voice, so to speak, I reflected on this. Suddenly it was really important to me to speak up. I feel I regained my ability to communicate, because I have important things to say.

And so, six years after I started writing this, I dusted off the first 3 chapters, which I had started and put down many, many times, then kept going. I didn't stop until I finished. It was painful, and painstaking.

Progress was extremely slow. I learned all about grace. The tears welled up as the letters appeared one by one, and blurred my words on the screen. I took a deep breath and reminded myself that this is important. I wiped the tears and continued, for hours quite often into the darkness of night wearing sunglasses, with the brightness turned down because light sent shooting pain to my eyes. I persevered.

I didn't know if I'd have another stroke, a much bigger one. This could be my last chance to tell my story.

The most important thing to me at this point is to pass on what I went through, what I survived.

So that you know you aren't alone in what you have endured.

Life was hard, but it was so beautiful.

My right eye didn't recover fully. We've seen in the scans that the blood supply is blocked by a clot. This doesn't get better apparently. It's a year on and it only clicked when I had another TIA recently and I lost a bit more focus that it wasn't suddenly going to get better one day.

Yet along with that blurring of my sight, which is not corrected when I use glasses or contacts, colours changed in one area of my vision, and it really was so spectacular. My eyes hurt, I couldn't watch TV or look at my phone, it was too bright.

But it was so very beautiful.

Like a door had opened into another world a tiny bit.

And so, my first stroke was not a huge one, but it was enough to mess me around and change my life, and my husband's.

I need to have heavy anticoagulants now, forever. I have no choice, so of course this means that it just isn't practical to live the way we live now.

I can't play with chainsaws anymore (boo!), If I cut myself, I could bleed out. This illness is nasty. I could stroke again anytime, even on the medication and I've spent the last year learning to be ok with that. It's very hard, but It's necessary to move to be closer to a hospital. I think I only managed so well last time because I was right there, a minute away from a scanner and medics. If one that scale and duration happened again, here at our home It would likely be a different story.

There are other types of strokes known as Transient ischemic attacks (TIAs), these are small, sometimes unnoticeable, they are known as the silent strokes, and I've lost count how many of these there have been. So, as I write this our place is currently for sale and were moving back into a town, a little less reclusive and only a few kilometers to hospital if I needed it.

Of course, with all this chaos going on, naturally I've reflected on my life. I've flitted back and forth about how I feel about not having my children here, now that it turns out that my health is absolutely shocking. Would it be fair if I had all my children living their lives constantly worrying about Mum?

No, absolutely not.

And then thinking of them, and not me, could it actually be for the best, in the big picture that my babies left me before they were born? Unfortunately, at this stage. Yes.

Horrific for me to have gone through what I've gone through in the journey of loss with each of them, but for them, maybe that's the reason why.

If I'd had children, I'd have wanted to give them my absolute everything. All of my attention, spent time learning with them, playing, baking, reading and generally just being the best Mum I could have been.

I wouldn't have been able to do all the things I'd have wanted to, and they would have suffered because of my disability, through no fault of my own -or theirs. That would be awful for them. Something I've learned this last year: life is almost defined by the fact that it is ever-changing.

CHAPTER EIGHT
Legs in the stirrups please.

2003

I think it's time to lighten the mood here. Let's briefly go into what you can expect as a lady whose plumbing is a bit dubious, and you want to have a baby. You're going to have to see doctors, and they're going to have to see you.

Recently a good friend of mine has had some pre-cancerous cells show up on a smear.
She had them cauterized but it didn't work so she had to have loop therapy and cryotherapy.
She remembered that when I was nineteen, I had to have this, so she called me and I told her

roughly what to expect, how long for recovery and so on.

After her procedure she called me again and told me about the medical students. It came flooding back!!! I hadn't warned her that all young doctors have to learn. They have to look and take notes so that they can become fabulous pioneers of the future!

Back when I was just nineteen, I'd had some pain and weird irregular bleeding. They'd done a smear because they'd ruled out anything else and it had come back with dodgy cells. Over the next three years I was cauterized six times and these cells just kept coming back positive for pre-cancer.

So, I opted for loop therapy. This is where they use a fine metal wire loop, they inject your cervix with local anesthetic, and they basically remove a few millimeters of your cervix in a slice. They use the hot thing after to stop the bleeding. You're basically sliced with cheese wire. It's really not a nice experience but the alternative is developing cancer, so.

Any gents reading must be feeling very relieved to be gents right about now.

Anyhow, I'd been back and forth for cauterization, and this was the big day, they were looping away some of my cervix.

The nurse helped put me at ease and I slipped into one of those sexy cotton shapeless granny gown numbers and she popped my legs into the stirrups and very gently placed a lovely warm blanket over me. I waited for the consultant to come in and see me before they knocked me out.

In he comes, fine specimen of a chap. Very 'tally ho' and all that sort of thing. Probably went to Oxford or similar. Very jolly and not a terrible bedside manor actually. Which is more than I can say for some of these geriatric doctors who were trained in the fifties who still think all females are 'hysterical' if they say they have lady pains.

Then, at the end, he's about to have me anaesthetized when he quickly asks, hand on the door, on his way to scrub up,

"I've got a couple of med students shadowing me today, your case is interesting, would you mind if they came in and had a look through the microscope so they can learn?"

Now by this point, I'd already had six cauterizations in three years. Countless doctors and nurses had seen my hoohoo. Although it was never a calming or relaxing thing to do, I always say yes because they do have to learn and I'm all for that.

"Absolutely! Of course I don't mind."

I laid myself back again, and in they come... blinking twelve of them!

White coats, name tags, clipboards in tow and
hungry eyes, desperate to look inside my vagina
through a microscope. To scrutinise my dodgy
cervical cells which were about to be
obliterated.

I could have cried as eight male and four female
trainee doctors, one by one, put their faces
within a foot of my private area.
They'd scribble some notes then move along
the line so their overly keen peers could get 30
seconds uninterrupted view of pre cancer
through a scope on a real live person.
It really was something else.

Only one of these lovely students said thank
you. I thought that was nice of him initially.

Then it dawned on me that perhaps he hadn't seen a vagina before. Perhaps my lady bits were the first ones he'd ever seen in real life.

You see, in the madness, the lines blur and the mind wanders...I wondered about these young people, would they get together over lunch that day to discuss said hoohoo? I don't know, perhaps it was the premeds kicking in?

Off they went back out the same door they came in and the anesthetist asked me if I was ready. My response was only part in jest.

"If they come in a flock like that for the next person, please offer to put the poor soul to sleep first."

What can you expect when you'll never be expecting?

You can expect that many medical people are going to want to 'look' at you.
In my honest opinion, I've learned that it's best to detach body from mind at the door for this stuff. Mentally hand over your body at the door of the hospital and just accept that, while you're there, it isn't your own. You can collect it at the pharmacy on your way out.

CHAPTER NINE
The margarine tub

2004-2010

TRIGGER WARNING FOR GRAPHIC DESCRIPTION
OF MISCARRIAGE, SUICIDE AND SELF HARM.

I haven't gone into too much detail regarding
the actual physical loss of a baby so far. I sort of
don't want to. If you're reading this because it's
happened to you, then you'll fully understand
why I don't want to take the rawest, most
painful box and open it wide. However, writing
this is supposed to be healing for me, and
informative for you. So, needs must. This
chapter covers graphic detail about the physical
side of miscarriage. Go to the next chapter if
you want to avoid it.

Still with me? Right, here we go.

As women, we are united by the things we have in common, but I've learned that we can become divided by our varying experiences. Suffering a miscarriage bonds us to those who have experienced it, separates us from those for whom it is never more than a silent fear.

It can be hard to tell the moment something goes wrong in a pregnancy. Unless it's because of something like a fall, or trauma from a car accident. Often we don't even realise that something so shattering has occurred.

My experience: I went for my scan, and I had presumed everything was fine. I'd had no pain, I still had morning sickness, my breasts were still really firm and sore, and my ankles were feeling like they had heavy weights on them, so puffy and tight. I lay there smothered in gel in the darkened room while she ran the little thingy over my tum and then there was a silence where there should have been chatter as she did a quick couple of measurements, clicked the computer a few times, and asked me if I'd like to see my baby. Silence.

"I'll be back in a sec, Chloe."

My heart sank. Fear and panic crawled up my throat as if to strangle me. Please, no. Not again. I lay there praying she'd needed the loo or something.

No. She returned with the doctor in tow.

And I knew exactly what he was going to do, and what he was going to say.

He quietly and politely says hello to me. He goes over to the screen with her, they look, he nods, like some unspoken code. He takes more gel, goes over my tummy again with the thingy, squints, and stares intently at the screen, and then it happens.

He's seen enough, he's seen this before. So have I.

He's seen this before, in one in four.

One in four but always bloody me.

He swivels his chair back, grabs me some paper towel for the gel on my tummy, he flicks the lights on, pulls the chair in slightly closer, and he says it.

"I'm really very sorry Chloe, your pregnancy is no longer viable, there is no longer a heartbeat, by the measurements today I'd say it stopped developing maybe a couple of weeks ago. I'm sad to tell you that you have miscarried. It's best to wait 3 months before you try again."

The universe goes dark. Your world crumbles to dust. The world you've built of your desperate half-belief that this time it would be different. Now you have around 5 or 6 minutes to take in some general information from the nurse about what your body will do over the next few days, you get dressed and then you're out the door on your way home.

That's it.

You just go home.

At this point I should tell you to always take someone with you to these scans. Don't go alone, if there is an issue you really don't want to be by yourself when you're told your baby has passed away or that there's a complication. You want someone you love and trust, to have a hand available to hold, just in case. Definitely during the first 12 weeks.

In that first trimester anything really can happen.

Sometimes we go home with an empty tummy because it left us already. Our baby, our fetus. There is different language according to when it happens. Up until 6 weeks there's no heartbeat yet so the Doctor considers it a bunch of cells.

After 6 weeks we have a heartbeat and a "viable pregnancy". After 12 weeks the doctors refer to your baby as your baby, but up until that point there are many names: pregnancy, fetus, embryo, but for me, as soon as I found out I was pregnant, the tiny life inside me was already my baby, *my child*.

Sometimes we go home with our baby still inside us and we must "let nature take its course." This means you go home, wait for the cramps and bleeding and you manage it yourself. You might pass your baby in the bathroom while you're at home, or at work, or while you're walking the dog. Some women have to carry on as usual; they still have to continue taking care of their other young children while they're going through this. I didn't, obviously, but many women do. I have had a miscarriage, put a pad in my underwear and passed my baby sat at my desk at work the next day. I passed one in the bath. I had one on an airplane. Sometimes you can't carry on as normal. Sometimes it's not just like bad period cramps. Sometimes it's absolutely cripplingly painful and you scream. It's horrific.

Sometimes the "pregnancy remains" get stuck. By this I mean nature does not take its course. For some reason, your body doesn't let go and you have to get a medicine that will open your cervix and move things along. A mini labour if you will. Sometimes even that doesn't work. In this case, a small surgery is needed, it's known as a D&C, *dilate* and *curettage*. They put you to sleep and remove your miscarried baby. I had to have this. Of course I did.

Sometimes you bleed a lot, sometimes barely at all. Sometimes you can see your tiny embryo and sometimes it's mixed in with the blood loss and you don't see it. Sometimes you feel the baby slip through your cervix, and sometimes you get a missed miscarriage, when there actually is a blighted ovum, for some reason the egg sac is totally empty and doesn't form inside at all, but all of the signs of a pregnancy are there, including a positive test, it's just that nothing forms. Occasionally it can be an ectopic pregnancy, this is really incredibly sad. The egg and sperm meet inside the fallopian tube and stay there rather than embedding in the uterus wall. It's extremely dangerous for the mum and continuation of that pregnancy will result in the loss of the baby, and probable death of the mother. A baby cannot grow in that tiny tube. It doesn't stretch like a uterus, it ruptures. The mother will have to have the fallopian tube removed, along with her baby which is inside. The alternative is bleeding to death.

So, we all are vastly different, with different circumstances, different types of miscarriage, at different stages of pregnancy, but the one thing we all have in common is pain. Emotional and physical. This is a difficult book to write and I imagine it's very difficult for you to read. I'm not sure but at this stage you may well be putting it down in order to go and scrub out the rabbits hutch, rearrange the fridge, disinfect the kitchen bin or literally anything else could be a more desirable thing to do than carry on reading my mopey chapters. So, time for a borderline-inappropriate funny story. Yes, I think so.

Funny, mortifying and 100% true, like all the best comedy.

I attended my GP's surgery daily for blood tests for a short period of time and this was not an easy feat. I'm a slow bleeder. Simple as that. I always try to donate blood every year sometimes twice a year and I noticed after a decade of donating that when I was coming in through the front doors of the donation center, the regular staff recognized my face and suddenly started to busy themselves with other people. I'd sit and wait my turn and inevitably I eventually got palmed off onto an unwitting new member of Staff who would then spend the next 45 minutes sweating, shaking and getting flustered because he was not able to get the blood out of my vein. It wasn't his fault: this was a common thing.

The nurse at my doctor's surgery knew this. She'd booked double appointments every morning for a week and this was the third day I'd been there. I'd done everything I was supposed to do. She told me I should drink water as soon as I got up to stay hydrated because it would help my veins and then when I got to the doctor's surgery, she immediately had me put my hands into a sink of hot water to get the little blighters up to the surface. Still today they wouldn't show themselves, the defiant little cretins. The nurse gave me a stress ball to squeeze to get my blood going. My eyes wandered around the room whilst she tapped at the hiding vessels, trying to gently coax them out. At some point I dropped the stress ball and it rolled across her office floor. She said not to worry about it, to just keep opening and closing my hand. I was tucked in front of her with my arm outstretched veiny side up on a pillow on the corner of her desk.

She reached to unpackage the needle, so I turned my head away and let my eyes wander around, I looked at the poster on the wall about food groups, my hand still obediently opening and closing. I noticed that under her desk her handbag had a Disney key chain on the strap, and there was a photograph next to her computer, presumably of her grandchildren.

My cold pale hand was still palm up, opening and closing as instructed while she poked around my inner elbow. It was starting to ache, so I was squeezing my muscles harder now. I turned away again and gazed out the window. Then it happened. I was opening and closing my hand, using all my might because my digits had gone all numb and as she leant over to reach for the vial, her enormous bosom somehow landed in my hand, and I squeezed. Hard. She yelped and sat back, and I apologised profusely. I'd squeezed her poor boob with all of my might! I was not laughing, I felt so embarrassed.

However, on the way home, the giggles came, they turned into an absolute belter of a laugh and as I walked back down the long road towards my house, drivers in the passing cars must have thought I was on day release.

You have to be able to laugh at life from time to time, laughter warms the heart and heals the soul they say. So, if nature sends you a ginormous and loud fart which just doesn't seem to ever stop, or if there's an accidental boob grab, just go with it. If life's giving you comedy amidst the drama, take it.

Why? Because the sheer, crushing, hollow disappointment of miscarriage is heavy. The deep sense of loss and sadness, that feeling of emptiness.

All of us one in four had sat and talked about nursery colours, and names. We had looked at prams, we had made plans. We had wondered who our children would be, the tiny being in our belly, who would they become as they grew? *We were already mothers*, and our plans and hopes and dreams were snatched away from us.

One of my dreams was fully immersed in icy water late one February.

Medical people all look the same after a while. The scrubs come in assorted colours with the different jobs they do. Once you've been into the ER few times, you might recognise a couple of faces, but you're rarely treated by the same Doctor, not on the NHS in the UK at least. The staff turnaround is pretty high. People move departments as they go on with their own lives and careers, so it's not often you'll be seen by the same medic. It's easy to feel detached and lost in this environment at the best of times. I can feel the warmth of these people, that's how I distinguish between the staff. If I go into the emergency department, I don't remember names or scrubs or titles of the profession. I don't really recall whether they are a health care assistant, or a registrar. What I remember is their warmth. I recognise the staff who looked into my eyes last time, who spoke softly to me, who held my hand or offered to call someone to collect me in my hour of imminent loss.

I rarely remember the others. The ones who spoke to me like they were reading from a script. Androids. I remember all of their words, but not their names or faces.

Apart from one.

He was a Consultant Registrar on the gynecology ward.

It wasn't my first miscarriage. I had found out weeks before that I was pregnant and had no end of issues since. Pains, intermittent bleeding, trips back and forth to hospital for checks, and I was only 8 weeks pregnant when I started bleeding. I had gone to the hospital, and they had told me I'd miscarried one of my twins, but the other remained and seemed to be doing simply fine. I had to keep going back each day for blood draws to check that my pregnancy hormone level was still rising, and it was. I was desperately clinging on to the remaining twin and everything was going well for the next month, until the pain.

The pain was sharp, really sharp, like a hot stabbing pulling feeling and there was blood, I'd woken with it, and I noticed blood when I went to the loo. I came back to the bedroom, and I saw it, there on the bed.

The dark red stain screamed at me from the middle of the white Egyptian cotton bed sheet. It looked like a shroud. I realised that if I hadn't already lost my remaining twin, it probably wouldn't be long.

There was just too much blood.

Nick was home that day, so I woke him up, it was just after 6.30 am. I turned on the lamp and gently shook him, I told him we had to go to the hospital, that I was in pain, that I was bleeding. He sighed and rolled over, told me he couldn't come, he couldn't cope. His mother had unexpectedly passed away 6 months earlier and he had been depressed, everything was on a steady decline. I'd only got pregnant this time because he told me in no uncertain terms that he wanted children. He wanted them now, he didn't want to be an old dad, and if I couldn't give him children, then...

And he never actually said it, he never finished that sentence. He left it hanging there. It was unsaid, but it was absolutely there. Later that day when it was calm again, I went and asked him. "Did you really mean it Nick? If I can't give you a baby, you'll go? And he shrugged his shoulders, sighed, looked up at me and replied, "I don't want to be an old dad, Chloe. I want them while I'm young."

It was unsaid, but it was said, and heard, loud and clear.

So, this was the second twin I was potentially losing, it wasn't just a loss for me. For us. It was game over. I kind of felt how Henry the VIII's wives might have felt, provide me an heir or, well not off with your head, but definitely out the door you go.

I called a cab to the hospital. I grabbed a black bag from under the kitchen sink, so I didn't spoil the taxi man's car seat. This wasn't my first rodeo. He pulled up outside and I threw the bag on the seat and got in. I said, "I'm very sorry I need to go to A & E, I'm having a problem with my pregnancy" and he didn't bat an eyelid, I was there in what felt like ten seconds, and when I went to pay him, he wouldn't take my money. He was a kind man. Such moments of human kindness are a beacon in my darkness.

I went through the main doors and was swiftly pulled in for an ultrasound.

I received the talk, about what to expect, and actually I tried to take it all in fully this time because I hadn't got this far along before, I was 14 weeks and 2 days with twins, it was different, not much different but there was more to it.

The doctor told me to go home and rest, that nature would do its thing, I had to stock up on pads and keep a note of how much blood I was losing, in case of hemorrhage.

And it wasn't my first time, I'd seen my miscarriage at 9 weeks, held it in my hand, not knowing what the heck to do with it.

I asked him, "what should I do with it?" and genuinely he looked at me as if I'd asked him how to thread a needle with a house brick.

I was met with silence, and a curious squint. He was digesting what I'd asked him.

Other ladies might have kept their questions to themselves, they might have been too polite to ask, but it was a genuine question, I really didn't want to flush my baby down the toilet, and I didn't have a garden of my own to bury my tiny loss. So, it was a legitimate question.

He shook his head as if he didn't get it and I asked again, "This is my third, I don't want to flush my baby in the toilet, I've loved this baby since I found out these twins were inside me, what should I do with it?

And his response...

"If you want to you can save it, put it in something and bring it back here to us, we can dispose for you." and part of me felt something warm, some good, kind intention behind this clueless doctor's eyes. Another beacon.

"Ok, yes that sounds like a good idea, thank you. Thank you ever so much, it was so hard last time, knowing what to do with it, what should I bring it in?" thinking he'd give some kind of tiny box or something, and he said it.

"You can use an old margarine tub and bring it in, we can dispose of it in the clinical waste."

In the considerable pause that followed this remark I'll tell you that I've worked in hospitals, and I can tell you that clinical waste is everything from hazardous dressings soaked with disease infected blood, to diarrhea-stained bed sheets. It's the really awful hospital stuff that gets chucked in the sluice together, then in the hospital incinerator.

They don't say a few words before they switch it on, it's just flung in like trash.

It was at this point I picked up my handbag and walked my blood-stained pajamas out of the hospital room slamming the door behind me.

This baby ended up being the one that really didn't want to go. I didn't pass it naturally. I waited and waited and it didn't happen. Then I had a D&C but after a couple of months it became apparent a little bit of pregnancy tissue had been missed, it happens occasionally. I got an infection in the end and had to have a second small procedure to get me sorted.

Later, I talked to an undertaker friend of mine. He explained that they do a free service for miscarried babies once a week, they take them from the hospital to the crem and they have a joint service.

I don't know how true that was because it was different from what the Doctor had suggested, but I appreciated his kindness, even if it was a lie. I found out recently that he has now passed away. I'll always hold dear those kind words. It helped me to see my angels in a more beautiful place.

So, when I returned home from the hospital after 3pm that afternoon sobbing, and found my husband still in bed, I gently woke him and told him what had happened, and his words would forever ricochet in the depths of my soul.

He said "For God's sake Chloe, again??!! What the hell are you doing to them?!" And he sighed and got up and went to the little room to play Xbox.

That little room should have been the nursery where he played with our child.

I got into bed and questioned whether I should kill myself that night.

Two nights later I acted on those thoughts and was taken away by ambulance, after slashing my arms twenty-two times with a razor blade, drinking three bottles of wine, and swallowing a box of lithium.

And so here we are.

I understand the hurt and the feelings of inadequacy that you might be carrying around, the crushing weight of the emptiness inside, the trauma of seeing your baby inside the toilet bowl, or on the tissue, the questions:

"was it something I did?"

"Perhaps it wasn't the right time right now anyway"

You'll be all over the place, basically. Like I was, every single time. I've agonised over absolutely every detail, for years and years, you aren't alone, you aren't inadequate and I'm 99% sure that you didn't do anything wrong. I've felt your pain. Millions of other women have also felt your pain too. You aren't hopeless or worthless and you aren't alone. We are an enormous collective of people who have gone through a truly awful thing, and nobody talks about it. Nobody. I'd like that to stop, right here, right now. It's time we grew the hell up as a society.

You're going to be ok, but I wasn't anywhere near ok yet, and a big part of why I wasn't was my husband.

CHAPTER TEN
The Chocolate Teapot

A decade ago, I'd have said that my first husband, Nick, was useless.

Well maybe not useless, that's just unkind, but I would have said he was as useful as a chocolate teapot. I'd have said that he was obsessed with playing Xbox, and he was immature. He didn't eat with me, he didn't take me anywhere, he rarely even walked the dog with me. It was really not a good marriage.

To this day I don't know why he proposed. He spent barely any time with me, it was as if I was single or living with the invisible man. I lived in a house just surrounded by wedding photos. Some of my friends joked that he was made up, because he never came anywhere and they hadn't ever met him.

All of the above is undoubtedly true - but remember how I told you how I had a stroke, and something strange happened? I see the world differently now. Maybe because I'm not holding onto the anger, I see the past through wiser eyes.

The truth is, we were *so* young. We had an idea of who we wanted to be and how we wanted our lives to look, but we weren't those people yet. We were naïve, and unforgiving if something didn't go to plan. We were not able to communicate well and because of that the breakdown happened really, even before the marriage took place. He was eighteen, I was nineteen when we met. It was June. We were living together within 3 weeks. Nick had proposed within 3 months, and we were married in the following May. We were kids and we had absolutely no business playing house. Not even close.

I had come from years of instability at home, and I craved normality. I could write a whole other book on my home life instability. I've told you about my mother but there was far more to it. Safe to say it was intense and deeply damaging. She was not a good parent at any stage of my childhood. However when I was age 11 she moved in a boyfriend. The next six years my home was filled with every kind of abuse. There was a court case when I was seventeen and after many years, I'm doing great. but back then it's probably fair to say that when I met

Nick, I was a child. A hurt, broken child, even in my late teens and early twenties. I was damaged, and I hadn't developed the emotional skills needed for life. The instability had been so much and the moving around had left me unsettled. Things had been too chaotic for too long and although on the outside I looked like a normal grown woman, I really hadn't grown up in lots of ways. The truth is I needed a therapist, not a husband.

I was craving love, the love and nurturing of having my own family, and it never came. I was craving for my husband to whisk me up like Richard Gere and promise me that it'll all be ok, and it just didn't happen.

If you also are waiting for that to happen, stop.

It was never Nick's responsibility to fix me, mend me, make it all better.

It isn't anyone else's responsibility to fix your pain either. Not just about baby loss, but any kind of trauma. It's easy to blame those closest to us when things don't go our way, but the reality is those closest to you are there to live alongside you, by choice. It's nice to have someone to confide in, but they aren't there to be your therapist. You can't be theirs, either.

He adored me in the beginning, isn't that always the way? I was the shiny penny. I felt so special, but we were ill-equipped to deal with the complexities of marriage, let alone the heartache of loss. We didn't know who we were yet. We were still growing up, and as we grew I think we realised that we didn't have much in common.

Is that right? Were we just too young? I'm not so sure. I think it's more about emotional maturity. If you are a good match, and you know what you want and you have respect for each other, I think even from an early age it can work. I look at my grandparents, both sets married incredibly young and lasted forever, but they weren't brought up in a `throw away era` like us kids of the 80s were.

Nick was an only child and his mum had taken care of him. She had always taken such loving care of him that he couldn't even boil an egg when he left home. He wasn't prepared for married life. I think he was expecting his wife to just take over the role of Mummy (his mum was a lovely lady by the way) and that was exactly what happened. This was not my idea of marriage. I wanted someone my equal to share life with. I didn't want to be the little woman indoors, rearing the kids and baking cakes, cooking his dinner, washing his clothes.

That never was the dream for me, I wanted to be a nurse, he wanted to be a police officer. He took the entry tests three times and gave up on the third fail. I took a promotional exam at work and stepped up the ladder and got a raise, and my goodness, he resented me for it. He took out his own disappointments in life on me.

I'd always worked, as soon as I was legally old enough to work, I always did, and even a little before. Baby-sitting the neighbors little ones, I was a Saturday girl in a shoe shop, I was a waitress in a local café, and a pot wash in a local restaurant and I did the obligatory stint as a burger flipper, but got sacked when they found out I was not old enough to work there. I'd lied about my age to get the job; I was fifteen and still at school.

I've never been afraid of hard work.

In the early years of my life with Nick, I worked two jobs and studied full time to become a nurse. I was a mature student so in the day I'd study my full-time course, at 4pm I would leave and go on to my call center job until 8pm, and from there I'd hop across town to my pub job, where I'd be on my feet until closing time. I'd go home anytime from 11pm to midnight after my shift ended. I'd stink of beer after pulling pints so I'd come home, jump in the shower, shove the laundry in the machine and then stay up to do my coursework while I munched on a bit of dry toast, because not only did he never ever cook for me, or leave a plate of a sandwich or something. Anything. He was the kind of guy who would use the last of the milk, or the last scrape of butter, and put the empty carton in the fridge. He didn't know how to care about someone. Didn't have the consideration or compassion. I'd come home and he would be playing on his computer, and the house would be a tip and it irritated the hell out of me that he was so thoughtless. My homes growing up were often filthy. I had told him this and I said I never wanted my home to be so dirty now that

I'm grown up. He obviously didn't care. It bred resentment.

I was constantly disappointed that my life wasn't how I thought it would be and I blamed him. I did my bit. I worked hard and he treated me unkindly. Like I didn't matter.

He never took me anywhere. Not out for a drink or out for lunch. I'd work all week and study as well and the weekend would arrive and he'd want to just sit in a room with the curtains shut playing war games on his computer. He'd be shouting and swearing into the headset at strangers, somewhere across the globe, who also sat in darkened rooms playing war games and no doubt shouted back at him.

So, I'd arrange to go out with friends, I'd invite him to come, he never did.

If you asked him about why the marriage went wrong, he'd say I was out with my friends all the time drinking, and he'd tell you I have mental health problems.

What he won't tell you is that I worked myself into the ground.

Working, studying, trying to keep a lovely home, trying to balance the rent and bills and on top of that I was struggling with the losses of our babies. When he said I was drinking too much, it was absolutely true. I was.

If even occasionally he had come to me and said, let's snuggle together tonight with a film and a pizza, I would have rather stayed home and done that. I didn't want to stay home in a room alone all the time by myself, eating by myself, watching films by myself, listening to him shouting into his headset from three rooms away.

I didn't want it. I couldn't stand it, so I'd go out. I wanted to live life. He wanted to close the curtains and hide from it and immerse himself into another reality.

He was an absent husband, and he struggled to be faithful, which was just another constant reconfirmation to me that I was inadequate. I tried hard to be a good wife, I loved him, but I felt `short changed` from the very beginning I suppose. When we'd been living together for 2 months, I was working and studying and doing all of these things, and what did he do? He quit his job. He came home and explained he didn't like it and it made him unhappy, so he had quit.

We weren't even married at that point, and I should have ended it then. As soon as he said it, I stayed outwardly calm but inside I was seething with anxiety. Maybe *he* had never had these worries before. Perhaps *he* never had to be concerned where rent money came from.

I had.

I did not crave a fancy expensive life. I did not have ambitions of my kids in clothes from baby GAP and I don't have a penchant for designer handbags. I wanted more for my children than I had for myself. Everybody does. My dad is a great dad, but it was the 80s and our mum got custody after they divorced. As much as he might have wanted to have us live with him there was only so much he could do. She even took us out of the country for a few months, He couldn't stop her despite getting a solicitor involved. Dads didn't have rights then like they do now. Our Dad always provided and paid child support, but it would go on gin, or a new outfit for date night. He came every single weekend to collect us on time and he always returned us exactly when he was supposed to. Not a minute before though. He literally wanted every minute with us that he was allowed. He never took us back late. He also never took us back early. We would sit in the car down the street and chat if we arrived a few minutes before we had to be back.

I had grown up moving from house to house, often in the middle of the night. My brother and I had been hissed at viciously by our mother as small kids to "shut up!" And "hide!"

Hide behind the sofa from the rent man, sky man, catalogue man, loan man, gas man etc.

I wanted my children to play freely out in the front yard without me having to dash outside and yank them indoors by the arm to hide from the people who had not been paid.

I would never quit my job without another to go to because frankly, I would not have done that to my husband. Maybe I sound like a martyr but I just wouldn't do that. I wouldn't load onto him all of the weight and burden and stress and worry which should be shared between us. If

171

one stops working through illness that's totally different, but just because you don't like it? No. Not me. In my mind I wanted to have enough income to cover rent, food, and bills. Extra was a bonus and not a necessity, but him just quitting threw us off instantly. A few weeks later, sure enough, we were short on rent. I was stressed, he'd been playing computer for the last month while I'd been trying to do it all and become a nurse all at the same time.

I'd had enough. I told him to pack his crap and clear off back to his mother. He was stunned. I still can't understand why he was so surprised. We'd rented a place that needed both of our salaries to afford. By doing what he did he'd screwed me over royally.

After a month he still hadn't managed to find a "job that he liked". I picked up overtime so didn't turn up as often to Uni as I should, and I never did get that nursing degree. I had longed for it since I was a little girl playing with my plastic nurses playset. Instead, I became a drop out.

I'd worked so hard through the years. I'd dragged my backside from the gutter to a moldy rented home. I was committed enough to my first job as an office junior to be promoted twice in 18 months, and left that firm as assistant payroll manager. For a big and well thought of company. I'd had to scrape my way by, always. I genuinely don't think he ever had.

His family life and upbringing was very different from mine. His Dad and Mum were together, his dad worked 12-hour days as a builder 6 days a week to earn for them. They'd never needed to hide from the gas man. Why couldn't Nick do that for me? How the hell could he think it would be ok?

I was never spoiled and I'm not greedy. If I'd had children, there'd have been no expensive birthday parties for my one-year-old with a pony dressed as a unicorn at a grand a pop. That's not me.

But, I needed the basics. Needed to know they were taken care of. Especially since we wanted a family. I think Nick presumed money just floated in each week and it doesn't.

Children cost money.

I needed the basics and he couldn't give them to me, or understand my need for them.

We were not compatible.

Over the next decade, bit by bit we came to fully resent each other and picked each other apart until there wasn't much left of either of us. That's the truth.

Neither of us was entirely to blame. We both had our moments of being a bit childish, and I'm not proud of some of the things I did and said. When it came down to it, we were just kids, playing house and ill equipped to cope with the realities of life.

He lost his mum, unexpectedly and he just didn't really ever come back from that slip of depression. It hurt me too, her loss. I still to this day think of her and I can hear her beautiful vivacious laugh. She was a bit of a surrogate to me since I hadn't got a brilliant relationship with my own mother. I felt it too. I loved her deeply.

I tried to support him, but you cannot help someone who doesn't want to accept help. He just wanted to hide playing on his computer.

Even the strongest of couples would struggle to stay together after so many disappointments and so many shattered dreams.

At the time when he left, I was in therapy twice a week and on medication which left me quite sedated, so I was unable to work. I got barely anything in benefit help. I got £400 a month, and the rent alone was £600. Bills were extra.

There was also the question of £17,500 in credit card debts and loans from our joint account. I was aware of 5k of it, however these were the days where you put a written signature on the applications. After he had left I asked the bank for documentation because I had only joint signed on 5k.

They provided the papers with a signature that looked like mine on a joint loan... for £11,500.

I was left in dire straights.

He was young, but it wasn't just that. He wasn't a nice person and that's the truth. Nobody should call their wife a fat c**t ever, and he did. Regularly.

CHAPTER ELEVEN
Pity Dinner

2005

I have to be very cautious where and when and how I talk about being childless. If it feels pressured I just can't. I can't open up and talk about it to people when I don't feel a warmth with or a connection with them. If they've had a similar experience that's different: I'm happy to go through my own pain and sit and listen to theirs if the sharing of grief is helpful and healing. I'm pretty much always happy to share actual knowledge, or experience.

However, I absolutely refuse to share my private agony and get pitiful looks in a social context, particularly if I feel ambushed.

I was at a dinner party in my early twenties and after an hour or so, the host asked me, out of the blue: "Chloe, you lost your baby recently, how are you doing with that now?" It was followed by the head tilt. What kind of question was this? Another bloody hand grenade, that's what.

Some people are too cruel for words. She was just trying to make herself look good. I felt like the prey in the braying hunt of her fake pity. I couldn't escape. I couldn't leave without it looking like I was making a fuss, so I had to stay but oh, how I wanted to slap her stupid face. I felt fooled, ambushed. I'd been had. I wanted to push her off her chair and stab her in the chest with one of her antique fish knives.

I'm not violent, at all, but I genuinely at that point was still too weak to stick up for myself. Too meek to say no, too polite to tell someone stepping way over the line to simply "stop it". So, I answered her hideous questions, but Jesus H Christ, what the hell? I realised, too too late, that I'd been invited as a hot topic being displayed as a show piece, getting smothered in public pity.

I just knew when she was on the phone inviting the other guests she would have said "I'm inviting Chloe, she has had a terrible time and it's just nice to invite her you know? I'd like to cheer her up." It was the worst kind of virtue-signaling, spread over a three course meal, with me as a novelty centrepiece. She might as well have put an apple in my mouth and a sprig of rosemary up my derrière. May she rot in a hell where there's no Gousto deliveries.

Of course, what I should have done was pinned her on the floor and shoved every single bread roll into her stupid mouth so that she'd just for the love of God stop talking.

The other guests sat and listened and oohed and aahed as I twisted in the wind. She asked the questions as if she had taken notes from an agony aunt on daytime telly. It was awful and I couldn't pour the wine down my neck fast enough. I wasn't sure whether I'd start crying, in front of these people. I mean really crying with the snot and everything dripping on her beautiful white Harvey Nicks linen tablecloth, or whether I'd grab the steak knife and just take the bitch out. Screw you, Felicity. Screw you. How could she? I thought she was my friend.

Rescue came in the form of dessert: I was struggling with borderline diabetes at the time, so I stopped just short of staying and tucking into the meringue deliberately to ruin her lovely dinner party... (diabetic coma usually puts a spanner in the works at a party). I managed to leave with that excuse rather than sit through another two hours of coffee and drinks. I felt profoundly alone: not just because Nick never came with me to anything. I felt alone because she'd made me different. The other guests, who I barely knew, were fine. Nobody was going to pull them apart that night. They wouldn't have to defend themselves when they came up against an ambush dressed up as compassion.

I wish I'd had someone with me.

CHAPTER TWELVE
Nature vs Nurture

2008

I reckon it's fair to assume that while you're trying for a child of your own, you may end up thinking about what kind of parent you're hoping to be. You almost inevitably find yourself reflecting on your own family upbringing.

If your own beginnings were healthy and good and balanced, it might be something you don't even consider. You've got positive experiences to model your own parenting on.

But if there's a hint of instability in your own background, that can make it very different. It can change the way you look at everything.

I wanted children, but when I first found out I was pregnant, I was scared. It was a massive thing, and I had a lot of questions. My vagina might not let it come out. It might not stretch enough to give birth. Have you heard the horror stories? They're terrifying! However, the last person I was going to ask was my mother: we are estranged. Although she had reminded me every birthday that I'd ruined her. That she'd needed 200 stitches and I had her in 36 hour labour. My family members have since reassured me this was in fact not the case. It was just a way for her to make me feel guilty for being alive every birthday.

Anyway her stories oscillated in my mind ever since the first time she told me, and I was scared. Really afraid.

It's actually the only time my ex husband spoke sense. He told me regularly to cut her off, that she was toxic. He saw it way way back, long before I actually took the decision to do it.

It's been ten years now since I told my mother I couldn't have her in my life and to never contact me again.

It was an entirely necessary act of self-protection. I've never regretted it, not once, and I'd do it all over again if I had to. I wish I'd done it sooner, truth be told. She was terribly toxic.

Remember that I told you that she informed me she had terminal cancer, and I had the stroke the next day?

It was a nightmare trying to find out what was going on. Concisely, nobody wanted to say, "it's all a lie Chloe, she hasn't got cancer."

So, nobody said anything. I didn't hear anything at all. I was waiting each day. Wondering if this is the day I'd get the call to say she had passed away. It was so stressful. I had to get my husband to phone my cousin and find out what gives.

Well, breaking news: she was absolutely fine. She'd come back from a fortnight in Sharm El Sheikh and wasn't dying, and nobody thought to call and let me know That's the kind of person my mother is. She allowed her children to believe she was dying. And she wasn't.

My mother never was *nice*. Wasn't kind or nurturing. She *was* neglectful, narcissistic, unstable and completely selfish. She took out her frustrations on her children, often in the form of beating us with the wooden spoon from the kitchen, or a bamboo stick from the garden. Our teeth are terrible because she didn't take us to the dentist for basic health care. As a child I had an ongoing issue with nits because she didn't take care of us. My step mum would use lice treatment on me at the weekends and the French lady down the road used to take me to her bathroom and wash my hair for me with medicated shampoo if I was really riffing around the other kids. Our clothes weren't clean, there weren't bed sheets on the mattresses and there weren't clean cups in the cupboard. They were all sat out on the kitchen worktop with mould growing in them. We had too many cats and not enough litter trays. I would come home from school, let myself in with my front door key as young as age 7 and my nose would burn from the waft of ammonia of the cat urine as I pushed the door open.

As a young girl a lot of the other mums stopped their children playing with me once they'd seen the social services car pull up every other month.

If one of the mums came to collect their daughters after they had come to my house, they weren't allowed to come back. It might have had something to do with the huge cloud of cigarette stink that hit them as my mum opened the front door to theirs.

It's an understatement to say this has left me with "some issues"!

Once I became pregnant, I was absolutely overjoyed, but also overwhelmed by a wave of terror. Never mind my vagina tearing, what about the really important stuff?

What if I'm not a good mum? What – horror of horrors - if I'm like *her*? I can have a sassy mouth sometimes if I'm stressed. Would I lose my temper and scream at my children like she did at us? Would I take out my frustrations on them? Would I decide one day that they needed to be disciplined better, and bring into the house a cane from one of the plants in the garden, to use on their beautiful young skin, to teach them a lesson?

Absolutely not, one hundred percent not. Of course I wouldn't and I know that deep down. I've spent all of my adult life trying as hard as I can to be the exact opposite of my mother, Because I learned from her how NOT to behave.

Doubts about myself and my capabilities as a future mum came up time and time again. Especially since my husband at the time, as I said previously, would have been as much help as a blob of melted chocolate. I hear he has four children now and he's been married and divorced twice. Apparently, he's lining up wedding number three. He gives those rings out like they're from Christmas crackers. I don't know what kind of parent he is to his children today, now that he's older. When we were together, I always worried about what kind of father he might be. Would he help? Would he be supportive, and could I rely on him to take over the career stuff while I had maternity time? No, it terrified me. I wanted my children, but I was really scared I'd be left in the lurch, left alone as a single mum and unable to call on my own mum for advice, support and – love. Love. The thing I never felt from her.

So, when I lost my baby that time, I had thought perhaps it was my fault. Perhaps it was my fears, my thoughts, maybe because it was inside my body it knew I had these fears, so it went away thinking it wasn't wanted.

Of course, that's absolute madness, and if you're having thoughts yourself that your own baby didn't stay with you because they didn't want to, STOP THAT. NOW. I can tell you, it's nonsense. Repeat after me: "It. Wasn't. My. Fault".

It's nature's way. If your baby left you too soon, it is because of a hiccup within the genetics, or the DNA, unless you're sinking a bottle of vodka each day and making your body inhospitable in some way, or with drugs etc. It's nothing you have done.

I find my garden teaches me simple wisdoms: you can sow ten flower seeds and not all of them will survive.

It isn't the flowers' fault, and it isn't your fault.

I just really want to say this again to you, my sweet reader.

It's not your fault.

So please don't beat yourself up anymore. You have had enough blows without adding self-flagellation to your causes of pain. It won't make you feel better.

TRIGGER WARNING SELF HARM

Another brief note, if you are self-harming at this point because you don't know how to healthily deal with the crippling stings of what you've gone through, please don't. Stop it now. My weapon of choice on myself was a razor blade. I did it in an area which could not be seen. My thigh looks like it's been wrapped in a ball of wool... the scars are terrible. I live in Spain now, and I can't wear shorts in public.

Yes, for a brief second it gave me some relief. A release of some kind, but it's not a healthy way

CHAPTER THIRTEEN
The stroke, the vision, and the meditation.

2023

When I came home from hospital after my stroke, I was optimistic that I'd be back to my normal self very soon. It'll just be a few days, I thought: but it didn't happen. Light hurt my eyes and I had to squint and wear sunglasses to see where I was going.

My balance was awful. I even needed help walking to and from the bathroom. I found it hard to focus on my phone screen and if I got a text the letters would move and jumble up. I simply couldn't read the words. I'd tire so quickly, be completely exhausted by a tiny amount of activity. Halfway through brushing my beautiful thick blonde locks, I'd have to stop and lie down.

This meant it got matted and after a month I had no choice but to take the scissors to it. It was heartbreaking.

Getting dressed in the morning was all I could manage. Even a month or two after, I would go to get changed and I couldn't work out my clothes. I wouldn't know what I needed to select and when it came to the actual act of getting dressed and undressed, I was doing things in the wrong order and getting in such a mess. I'd try to take off my vest with my cardigan still on and get tangled.

If it were cold, I'd wear thick slipper socks, but when I'd come to take off my trousers to put pj's on later, I'd end up cold because I'd take my jeans down, but they'd get stuck at my ankles by the socks. I'd be there in a heap, cold, not able to work out what to do to rectify this. Ordinary everyday things became nightmarish puzzles to be solved: sometimes they still are.

 Although occasionally I still get really upset if I'm not able to work something out, mostly I'm able to laugh at the difficulties.

The day I came back from hospital, I was cold. I asked Adam for some "gloves for feet" because I couldn't find the word "socks." Sometimes now, a year and a half on, if I go upstairs Adam might ask where I am off to, and I'll tell him I'm going to get some gloves for my feet, and we chuckle.

It's about perspective.

Another one of these:

If you are going through life and you won't ever be expecting, you can expect:

At some point, something will happen which will put everything into perspective.

After the stroke I found myself once again with a sense of emptiness and a lack of direction. I'd lost my identity again in a way, although I don't know if I had ever fully found it.

At this stage in my life, I sort of knew who I was.

I was a self-sufficient off gridder. I was a farmer, this was what I did. It was a full-time job and more. It wasn't a job; it was a way of life. It's who I was.

I'd spent two years settling into farming life, and suddenly I could no longer do it. It felt like when I had miscarried, a visceral loss. I was grieving the life I had come to love dearly.

My mindset has been everything on this journey. The way we see things is the way we feel things, isn't it? And feelings, emotions are so enormously powerful. I felt properly sorry for myself, and it wasn't healthy.

What had I done to deserve this?

I felt like I had been stiffed in the same way that I did when my dream of being a mother had been snatched away before. I'm a woman, and women have babies, and I'd had all the pain, the agony periods, the tender breasts each month. I endured all the lady stuff, but when the time came for me to have mine, I couldn't.

I felt robbed and it's partly to do with entitlement. I thought motherhood was my right as a woman, I just kind of expected it to happen. And when it didn't, I felt hard done by, and inadequate, and why me? Oh god, why me?

If I hadn't spent years just expecting to have babies, then it might not have hurt so much when it didn't happen.

It's all led me to some kind of epiphany, I suppose: we are not entitled to have children. They are a gift and if we are fortunate enough to be gifted with children then that is wonderful.

Having to stop living the off-grid life felt a bit like I'd had the carpet ripped from under me once again and although I tried hard to get back to normal, I did wallow in self-pity. It wasn't pretty.

I'd spent years, literally six years spending all my spare time researching, reading, learning, and taking in every bit of information on off grid living in preparation for our new adventurous life.

We had spent the last two years putting all that learning into practice and transforming our gorgeous 20-acre plot of Spanish land into a working farm. It was amazing. I'd not grown a tomato plant before and now I had seventy on the go out in the field. I had expected us to live out our days there, living that life.

It wasn't to be. A couple of months after the first, I had a second stroke. This one left me with a cerebral infarction. It's a polite term for saying I've been left with some permanent damage in my brain. I manage most things ok, but I do have to ask for help. I can't do dates, times, counting or working out certain things, like money in the shop or weights for recipes. Simple things, but important things.

Life looked similar. I looked similar on the outside, apart from my shabby self-chopped hair and slightly wonky face. But I wasn't the same and I struggled to adapt. Really struggled. I began to realise that life wouldn't actually ever be the same. I had to respond in some way, find some different way to react to this different life. This different *me*.

I turned to meditation as a way of keeping my stress levels down. I didn't think for one second anything would happen, I kind of thought perhaps it would encourage me to just have quiet time here and there for a more peaceful mind. But when I tried it, it opened something. In the same way the stroke opened something. It's hard to describe but my vision was affected after the first stroke. There was a change in colour in the upper right area of my right eye. I couldn't see clearly anymore through it, but I could see a patch of colour. It was like a portal to another place, another universe. For a while it was constantly there, like heaven had left the door open and they were waiting for me, if you believe in that sort of thing.

Meditation did something remarkably similar. It opened another portal, but one within. Trauma leaves us with noisy minds. My accumulated trauma – with which you are now very familiar - had left me with a constant, nagging noise in my head.

It was my own voice, and it never, never stopped. A running commentary on how useless I was and how I'd never be normal or deserve good things – but meditation soothed that right down. I was astonished. The quiet was almost shocking. I finally got out of my own head, my own niggly negative voice finally just shut the hell up for a minute and it was beautiful. I was quiet inside and out for the first time.

The wonder of it was only beginning. In the quiet, I could hear new things. It opened my mind and my heart to the sounds of nature. Mother earth was whispering to me somehow. This wasn't like me. A couple of years ago if someone said these things to me, I would have told them to shush their hippy mumbo jumbo, or less polite words to the same effect. One of them might have been "off".

The truth was that whatever was going on. *I felt calm*. My quality of life depends on how calm I'm able to stay. Tranquility and peace covered me like a blanket and with that came another epiphany: a massive shift in my own perspective. The way I saw life at that moment turned on its head.

Now, I understand. Finally, really, miraculously: *I understand*.

I`m not a biological mother, and I never will be.

It wasn't the way I'd planned it. I'd never envisaged my life without my own family.

With all I've been through, I've reached the point where I'm ok with that. You might not be yet, and that's ok. If you wanted children, and then it turns out that you really never ever will have them, you need to find a way to be ok with that. Otherwise, you spend your time fighting things you cannot change and that's just so draining, and ultimately self-destructive.

I know that no matter what happens, I can still live a rich and rewarding life, without having children, and so can you.

So really deep down, if you want to make the way you feel inside more comfortable at least...it's about finding peace on your journey, in unexpected ways I think. If you'd told me ten years ago to try meditation I'd have been skeptical and borderline offended.

We each find our own ways to soften the blows of life, and you *will* find yours.

CHAPTER FOURTEEN.
The Beginning

2024

This is the end of my book. Perhaps now you're asking how you can yourself feel better about your own situation. Some of you are probably thinking "Sweet lord is it going to take a stroke before I feel better?" and the answer is no, you'll be glad to hear! Of course not. It was a wakeup call for me and obviously I hope it never, never happens to any of you.

The crucial point for me was when we moved to our little farm and were living off the grid, doing all our self-sufficiency tasks.

It was very unexpected, to be honest.

We had moved here to live without bills, because I was already struggling to live a normal life with my adhesions problem. Day to day it's difficult to manage, the pain can be excruciating and unpredictable and I was struggling to hold down a job. So, we decided, let's do it all ourselves. Save as much as we can, buy a plot of land with a building, install solar, use wood from the forest to fuel the fire, collect rainwater and grow our own food and that's exactly what we did. On acute pain days I did what I could, and on good days when I felt well, I got really stuck in. And we did great, for almost 3 years we have been successful.

It never really was for the joy of growing vegetables or chopping wood, not really. We'd rather have been strolling hand in hand by the sea taking it easy, eating tapas in the evening. It was more about having the security of no mortgage. We were also craving peace and quiet after the Covid-19 pandemic. Of course, we have had to work ridiculously hard, and I saw all of the things in the beginning as tasks, chores, jobs. That once I'd done them then I could relax.

Even before the stroke, I'd noticed over a few months of growing plants and flowers and vegetables from seed that something was happening inside my soul. I can't put it any other way.

It was lighting up.

I couldn't wait to go outside and water my plants and see how much they'd grown since the day before. I was nurturing those seeds, tucking them into the compost which I had made with leftover veg and cuttings myself over the last year. I was feeding them, protecting them from the elements, and then they started to nourish me too. I got such a profound sense of achievement when I'd go out to harvest the beautiful fresh organic crops and bring them in and cook them that day or throw together a salad. I was harvesting 10kg of tomatoes each morning, and I couldn't get enough of it. There was such boundless joy in taking a basket of excess harvest and gifting it to a neighbor or taking it to a local bar for people to enjoy. We simply wanted to share our bounty. It was nice, and left me feeling fulfilled in ways I hadn't experienced before. I found real warmth and comfort in the tending of the plants in the nursery. So if you think it's not your thing let me tell you: it wasn't mine either! Believe it or not, I was a dolly bird in mascara with high heels and nail varnish and I didn't want to get my hands dirty. God forbid - but once I got my mitts in the soil, there was no stopping me. I don't know whether my hands were absorbing minerals through my skin from the earth, but it was a beautiful feeling.

And then I realised: this was me starting to heal. Quietly. Peacefully and privately out in the wilderness of the Spanish mountains.

Occasionally I'd kneel in the earth, deadheading my plants, or tying the crop supports, and the tears would flow down my face. My top would be drenched in tears, but it wasn't a painful type of sob. It was quiet, it flowed freely. I didn't attempt to stop it, or even reach for a tissue from my dungaree shorts pocket. My hands were filthy, and I didn't care. I tended my beautiful baby seedlings, whilst wiping snot and soil across my face, listening to the birds tweeting and the trees swaying. I didn't stifle my cries, the sky and the bees and the foxes and the forest didn't mind my sadness. I didn't have to use all my energy hiding my emotions. I think you know how exhausting that is.

I was free to live. Life. My life. I stopped trying to fill the uncomfortable silences where my children's laughter should have made a delicious cacophony on a Sunday afternoon. I stopped feeling sad in the evenings when I knew I should be bathing my babies. I'd go outside and tend my garden instead.

My stroke wasn't necessary for my healing. It just made me realise how short our time here can be, and I'd better start living and enjoying life. The truth is that I hadn't enjoyed a lot of my life by my twenties and by my 30s I was starting to feel like I wasn't invincible anymore.

None of us know how long we have here. My reality is that because of my illness my life could be cut short at any time.

I'd spent at least half of my life grieving, for my lost babies. I'd had a lot of stress and strain, and it was taking a toll on my health. One of my doctors has emphasised that stress is a problem for me and It's important to avoid it wherever possible.

I'd spent years fighting the reality that I couldn't have children. I kept trying and trying. With my older wiser and more experienced eyes I know now it wasn't meant to be, and it wasn't right to try to force it.

I accept myself fully now, just as I am. I am beautiful inside and out and I am strong. I have endured and this has made me a resilient person. I'm kinder to others. I am more understanding of other people's pain, because of my own.

So, what can you expect, if you will truly never be expecting?

You can expect the unexpected because that is life, my beauties.

You can try to prepare yourself, but the truth is it's your journey, and you're going to have to find your own way through.

I'm a 40-year-old survivor. I'm a survivor of abuse and neglect, miscarriage, suicide, typhoid, pulmonary embolism and many more life horrors. Any one of these things could have cut short my years. I feel like I'm the cat with nine lives - but I don't know when they're going to run out. I've been through so much and I've been incredibly lucky. How long can one be so incredibly lucky?

I never imagined I would be the person I am today, but I'm proud of who I am, what I've overcome. So never be ashamed of your story. Please, if you want to talk about it, do. Don't be afraid.

As I have, you might find it helpful to scribble your own hurts down. You don't need to show anyone. I only started my book because ten years ago I looked hard for a book like this, and there wasn't one.

There were hundreds of books about having children, being pregnant and breast feeding, but I couldn't find a book on NOT being able to have children. My husband was a psychiatric nurse, so I asked him about what help is available for people like me, today. It's been many years since my hysterectomy let alone my last miscarriage, so I wanted to find out what's new in the help side of things today. He said that the family doctor would refer the lady to his team for an assessment, so that they can work out whether you should go to a team who specialises in psychology, talking therapy, or you'd get bereavement counselling. It's no different from a decade ago.

Bereavement counselling isn't quite the right place for a lot of us. They discuss holding dear precious memories, treasuring special moments, focusing on the good times you had together. That isn't relevant to us, is it? We are grieving for everything we didn't get the chance to have.

Psychology might help, or talking therapy. Miscarriage is traumatic. Don't be afraid to ask for trauma counselling. Certainly as I mentioned earlier, EMDR is a treatment which really did help me to break down numerous traumatic events.

Really, you might just need some extra love, care and reassurance that you're OK.

If you're feeling suicidal because of your grief, then of course therapy will be part of your way out of that dark place. Medication short term can help you cope. It is entirely natural to collapse into dark despair for a while. Allow yourself to grieve but try to do it in bursts here and there. Otherwise, it's easy to fall in and get lost.

Rescue *yourself*. Don't stand there in the chaos waiting for someone else to make it all better. It doesn't work that way. This terrible thing happened to you. It hurt you, and nobody else can work on that, except you.

I know it can seem incredibly patronising when someone says, "you gotta do the work" and much as I detest that saying, it is true. You do. Nobody can do it for you.

Life may not be the life you we're expecting to live, but it is still your life. You'll find the beauty in it. Through your pain and suffering you might actually at some point appreciate that a life without children can also be fulfilling and beautiful.

I write children's books now, and I draw the pictures. I write stories for my own children, and then I publish them, for other people to read to theirs after they tuck them into bed at night. You can be maternal without actually being a parent.

Earlier, I said that I wasn't sure I had room in our life for children. All the way through this book I've said I'm not a mother. That's not true, we all can be mothers in other ways. I have a 24-year-old stepson who I love dearly. Being his 'bonus mom' as he calls me it's so enriching. I got to see him grow up from a 12-year-old boy to a remarkable young man. I can't wait until he has a family, and I can be 'bonus granny'. Not too soon though, I'm only forty. I'm a dog mama and earth mother too. I feed the birds and I plant the seeds. We all can nurture.

You can expect to build your own family if you want to. You can expect to need a strong partner so you can help each other through.

You can expect to have days where your pain is so bad you can barely breathe but keep going. Anniversaries will be hard. Due dates, dates you found out you were expecting if you were, the date you might have miscarried, and of course... Mothers Day.

Every time these dates come around; it hurts. Stings in the deep soul. Over time you'll find your own way to manage. On my dates, I do something nice that day. I go out, or I make something nice for dinner. I do something distracting, or I allow myself time to think and feel. It takes some pressure off. I don't know if these hurts ever go away, but they do become lighter to bear. I won't say it gets easier, or "time is a healer". I find these terms a little patronising and impersonal. Undoubtedly you become stronger. In the same way that if you carry a huge heavy handbag, your arm becomes strong. You carry this weight of feelings long enough and it doesn't become less heavy, but you gradually become more used to carrying it.

Planting a tree or rosebush can be helpful. It helps me.

You can still be important. You still have a lot to offer. Don't write yourself off just because your life isn't turning out as you hoped. Truth is, it rarely does.

I was right at the beginning. I do feel better for writing this, lighter. I hope that one day, you will feel lighter also, and less weighed down too, my dear reader.

Life is short. We never know how long it will last. If we didn't become biological mothers, it's because we are supposed to do something else.

Please don't spend your life engulfed in sadness.

Go forth, find your joy.

You're allowed to be happy.

Much love to you,

C.S. Fleur.

xx

Printed in Great Britain
by Amazon